HEALING MAGNETISM

HEALING MAGNETISM

The Transference of Vital Force

Heinz Schiegl

SAMUEL WEISER, INC.
York Beach, Maine

Original German language edition published by Hermann Bauer
Verlag KG, Freiburg, Germany under the title *Heilmagnetismus* von
Schiegl.
© 1983 Hermann Verlag KG, Freiburg

First English language edition 1987 by
Samuel Weiser, Inc.
Box 612
York Beach, Maine 03910

ISBN 0-87728-644-2
Library of Congress Catalog Card Number: 86-50197

Translated from the German by
Tony Langham and Plym Peters, Devon, England
Typeset in 10/12 Palatino
Printed in the U.S.A.

Cover mandala is a painting by Jeanette Stobie of Redwood City,
CA. © 1983 Jeanette Stobie. Used by permission.

CONTENTS

LIST OF ILLUSTRATIONS

FOREWORD

During my childhood it was customary in our family, at times of serious illness, to consult both our family doctor and our "family healing practitioner." He was consulted particularly when a member of our family had—for whatever reason—to undergo an operation.

In those days (the 1930s) the high risk associated with an operation was considerably more prevalent than it is today, thanks to the advances of modern medicine, especially in the field of surgery. However, even nowadays an operation should only be undertaken when it is absolutely necessary, not so much because of the techniques of surgery, but more because of the possible post-operative effects and other unforeseen consequences related to surgery.

Several members of my family owe their escape from the scalpel, if I may use this metaphor, to our healing practitioner. Not only did my grandmother and my sister escape in this way, but I, too, was saved from several operations by the natural healing treatments of our healing practitioner, as results were later to confirm.

However, having said this, nothing negative should be said about our family doctor. Our family physician was a general practitioner: nowadays one would refer to him as a doctor of general medicine. He was not presumptuous about his status, and he was, above all, a human being—a therapist such as there are very few today. His comprehensive medical knowledge, his experience, his way of relating to his patients, and above all, his kind manner when dealing with our anxieties and worries assured for him a confidence which many patients nowadays do not have in their doctors, though it is absolutely essential. It is generally acknowledged—and should only be mentioned here for the record—that our status-seeking society and our irrational attitude about health are the two principal causes of a miserable state of affairs in which even a doctor with the best will in the world is left with little time to deal properly with patients and their inner needs. In this context it is also important to note that our family doctor provided the commitment of his profession and the essential sympathy for the general well-being of his patients.

It was no secret in our family that in special cases our healing practitioner was also consulted almost as an "alternative" medical treatment. It happened more than once that two medical specialists would meet each other at the sick bed. Before giving our consent to an operation, the family doctor would be informed that we wished to try to bypass the (possibly) necessary operation by using natural healing methods. Our family doctor's true character revealed itself in such situations because he lent support to the patient through his attitude. Often he would use natural methods of treatment which one could apply in such cases. His motto was to try to exhaust all the possibilities—we can always operate later if we need to.

When our healing practitioner had cured the patient without an operation, our doctor would acknowledge this without any ill feeling, and even praise the treatment. I can remember that he once told me: "Natural healing is a good thing, too." With regret, he added, "Unfortunately, I don't understand enough about it as I was never taught its methods."

I must also praise our family healing practitioner, Ludwig Hirschmann, who has now passed on. As I grew older, this man was to become my friend and teacher. He possessed a vast knowledge of the extensive field of natural healing methods, and also knew a great deal about esoteric and related matters. In addition, he awakened my interest in alternative medicine. It was due to his inspiration that I became a natural healer myself. As a healer he was aware of his limitations. He would often advise a surgical operation or a traditional course of treatment because he knew where natural remedies could no longer help. The collaboration between academic medicine and the science of natural cures worked very well. The practitioners of both these disciplines had great respect for each other and gave each other the professional recognition that each expected.

When our natural healer made a house call it always struck me as being peculiar that, after examining the patient, or writing out a prescription, or giving instructions about therapy (frequently he would only advise home remedies, such as a cold compress), he made strange hand movements over the head and the whole body of the sick person. This seemed very odd to me at the time.

Later on, at the beginning of my undergraduate years, I frequently talked with Mr. Hirschmann. He had a small garden on the same plot of land where I had my own. I would often meet him there and was able to listen to his fascinating stories. It was there that I first heard about his achievements in healing magnetism and hypnosis, two of his favorite subjects. The burning interest which I already had in those two branches of the science of nature cures is still with me today.

Thus this book may be regarded as an expression of thanks to Ludwig Hirschmann, our family healing practitioner, from whom I have learned so much, and whom I would like to name as my first teacher in my career in the science of natural healing and nature cures.

Heinz Schiegl
February 4, 1983

Part 1

MAGNETIC THEORY AND HISTORY

We all have something of magnetic and electric forces in ourselves, and in the same way as the magnet itself, we exercise an attracting and a repelling force, depending on whether we are in contact with something similar or dissimilar.

Johann Wolfgang von Goethe

MAGNETIC THEORY

Most of us have, at some time or another, knowingly or unwittingly relieved someone from aches and pains by stroking our hand over the affected part of the person's body. This power, which nature has given to each of us in varying degrees of strength, enables us to remove pains and disorders from our own bodies. It also enables us to help other people, if we know how to use our power correctly.

Human magnetism is nothing new. It is a force in the form of a fluid energy which humans have been born with since the beginning of time. The subtle primordial element, also called *vital magnetism*, triggers off all our vital functions, such as movement, feeling, intelligence. In short, it is an energy that influences our senses, the metabolism, the building and growing of cells. It actually activates these processes. During the course of history, this mysterious force has been known under a variety of names which are all more or less appropriate.

Paracelsus recognized in it the magnetic fundamental force, or the so-called nature cure force, and called it *Mumia*. Mesmer called the remarkable healing force *animal magnetism*. In his honor, his friends and pupils introduced the expression *Mesmerism*. The geographer, Ritter, used the concept of *siderism*, a "theory using the influence of the stars upon health." The German scholar, Burdach, termed the healing magnetic process *neurogomy*, meaning "union of nerves." Reichenbach called it the *Od force*, and Klein called it *vital electricity*, while Professor G. Kieser coined the term *tellurism*, meaning "natural force of the earth." Other names like *vital magnetism, fluid energy, primeval magnetism*, etc., are also definitions of this force.

How does this force operate within a person, and what effect does it have? The human body consists of a very large number of individual cells which, apart from the blood cells, take the form of tissue. Tissue is a formation resulting from the division of cells of the same type. Depending on the specific function they are to perform, we can distinguish bone cells, cartilage cells, muscle cells, gland cells, nerve cells, blood cells and others. Most of these categories can be subdivided into different sub-categories.

Each individual cell consists of atoms, the true building blocks. The cells are alive; they form and renew themselves in a process called cell division. The force which carries on forming and animating these cells is called *vital magnetism*.

The difficult to imagine and, to us, mysterious course of all vital processes—the meaningful interaction of all the organs of the human body—is made possible only through the constant presence and influence of a force still invisible to us today. Vital magnetism consists of vibrations which are constantly present and which flow through the entire body. These bipolar—positive and negative—vibrations should always be present with equal strength to form a harmonious balance. They should be present everywhere, though nowhere too strongly. If the flow of vital magnetism is disturbed in any organ, or if one part of the organism is not fed by the necessary amount of fluid substance, a state of incomplete animation develops, and this state we call illness.

Since this vital energy can be transmitted from healthy to sick people, and this promotes the cure of many diseases, it has come to be known as healing magnetism. The transference of vital energy is known to large circles of people interested in the science of nature cures by this name, and therefore we shall use this term throughout the book.

The use of healing magnetism is as old as mankind. Primitive people exercised healing by following this instinct, upon which they could rely most of the time. In those early days, there were no chemists or doctors, and healthy people tried to help the sick by laying-on hands or by stroking and breathing upon the sick body. The best results were obtained when these methods went hand-in-hand with the strong wishes and goodwill of the person carrying out the treatment for the patient. Using these methods, some people produced very strong effects, obtaining results which were regarded as "miracles," since the healing could not be explained.

This may be the reason why, later on, healing magnetism was exercised almost exclusively by the privileged class of priests, and was guarded as a strict secret. The pronounced discipline and the remoteness of the priests from ordinary people—and above all, their claim to special powers—ensured that their knowledge of magnetic force was handed down only to those initiated in its theory, who in turn passed on their knowledge in the same way. The healing temples with their halls for the sick were famous, especially in Ancient Egypt.

In Europe nothing was officially known about healing magnetism and its effects until the Middle Ages. Only Paracelsus and his successor, Baptista van Helmont, came close to the truth. This is the answer van Helmont gave to the Jesuit priest Robert's fanatical condemnation of magnetic cures: "He who regards magnetic healing as the work of the Devil, must, by the same count, regard the causes of all magnetic phenomena as the magic of the Devil...." Undoubtedly van Helmont took care not to publicize the details of magnetic treatment, magnetic clairvoyance, or vital magnetism, though he had certainly researched these matters. According to the laws that prevailed in those times, he would very likely have been put to death at the stake for the Church was involved with the Inquisition.

Pope Innocent VIII issued a papal bull on magic, which resulted in the "Witches' hammer." This criminal code made it possible for thousands of innocent people to be condemned to indescribable torture and death by blind fanatics or vengeful enemies, even when there was no evidence against them. In 1678, the Archbishop of Salzburg had ninety-seven witches and magicians put to death. Apart from those falsely accused, many were mentally ill and were believed to practice sorcery. Even as late as 1749, Maria Renata, a nun who had lived for fifty years in a convent at Unterzell, was found guilty of witchcraft and was executed in Wurzburg. She was saved from death by burning by the Elector Clemenz, and died by the sword. Even so, her body was still thrown onto a funeral pyre so "that nothing at all would remain of the sorceress, and that even her brains would be lost in the ashes." In 1872, the last witch was burned in the Swiss canton of Glarus.

Today more and more people are interested in understanding the power given to the priests. Healing work is not just relegated to the priesthood—it can be used by all of us to better help serve humankind.

MAGNETS AND MAGNETISM

A magnet is a stone (ore) that has the remarkable property of attracting iron and, when suspended freely, sets itself in the direction of the magnetic poles. Every magnet has a north and a south pole. The force that produces this effect is called magnetism. For the derivation of the word *magnetism* we have to refer back to an earlier era because interpretations differ.

Pliny refers the name back to a shepherd called Magnes. The latter is believed to have been the first person to have discovered the magnetic stone using a stick coated with iron. According to Lucretius, the name probably originated with the Greeks in the region of the "magnetizers." Many people believe that its name came from Magnesia, a town or district in Thessaly where these stones were found in large quantities. Some called it *heraklion* (Hercules's stone). However, we regard the belief of the Hermeticists as the correct one. According to them, the word *magh*, or *magus*, was derived from the Sanscrit term *mahaji* ("the great one," or "the wise one"). This term actually referred to divine intelligence.

The priests traced their own wisdom back to the divine intelligence. Since they were also considered to be magicians, and derived their name from that word, the magnetic stone or magnet was so called in their honor, as they were the first to discover its magical properties. Their temples were found all over the country. Some temples were dedicated to Hercules, and that's why the stone was also called magnesia, or Hercules's stone, especially when it became known that the priests used it for magical and healing purposes.

Socrates (470-399 B.C.), one of the most important figures in Greek philosophy and of the Western way of thinking, remarked: "Euripides calls it the magnesia stone, but the people call it Hercules's stone." The country and the stone were named after the magicians, but the magicians did not derive their name from either of these.

In addition to attracting iron, the magnet was found to possess other remarkable properties, such as, the attraction of unlike poles and the repulsion of like poles, as well as the effect that magnets had on each other, even at a distance when they were not actually touching. This phenomenon was called "mineral magnetism."

A bar magnet suspended horizontally and pivoting freely, such as a compass needle, comes to rest in a north-south direction. The north pole points to the north; the south pole to the south. Since, according to the law of polarization, unlike poles attract and like poles repel each other, the earth's magnetic pole which is situated close to the geographical north pole is in reality a magnetic south pole.

The area surrounding a magnet is called its magnetic field. It can be illustrated by lines of force and can be seen if a sheet of glass is placed into the magnetic field and iron filings are sprinkled onto this. You can also create a magnetic field electronically by using a solenoid (see figure 1).

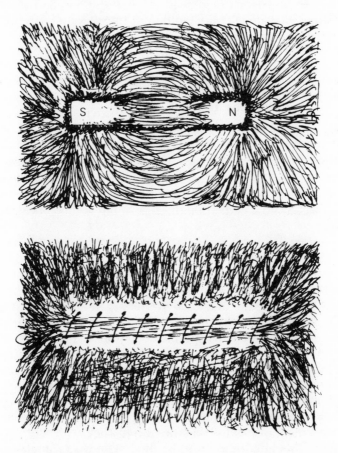

Figure 1. Top: The magnetic field of a bar magnet; Bottom: The magnetic field of an electric solenoid.

The German mathematician and astronomer, Carl Friedrich Gauss (1777-1855), who, with Archimedes and Newton, is regarded as one of the greatest mathematicians, discovered how the strength of a magnetic field can be measured precisely, and found a way to express this. Geophysicists use the letter "G" (Gauss) as a symbol for the unit of the density of a magnetic field. (For example, the earth's magnetic force has a density of 0.5 gauss.) Since time immemorial the magnetic field has been used for healing. However, these magnetic healing methods are in no way related to the doctrine of healing magnetism as described in this book. The treatment using the magnetic force field by means of the application of nature or electromagnetism is entirely different from healing magnetism, the treatment using vital or fluid energy.

Differences between Healing Magnetism, Hypnosis and Magnetic Therapy

Healing magnetism, hypnosis and magnetic therapy should not be confused; the effects of the therapies are entirely different. The most significant characteristic which distinguishes the treatments is that in magnetic healing, the transference of the vital fluid does not in any way influence or suppress the will. However, this does happen in hypnosis up to a certain point, and as far as the subconscious permits.

There are various definitions of the word hypnosis, but none of these really touches upon the essence of this valuable therapy. The most appropriate definition seems to have been produced by the British Medical Association in 1955. The committee defined hypnosis as "a transient state of altered awareness in the patient, a state which can be induced by another person and in which different phenomena can occur either spontaneously or as a reaction to verbal or other stimuli. These phenomena, of which the patient is not aware in his usual mental state, comprise a change in consciousness and memory, and heightened reception to suggestion, response and thought. In the hypnotic state, conditions such as anesthesia, paralysis, rigidity of the muscles and changes in the autonomic nervous system can be induced or suppressed."

Either with or without touching the body, the healing magnetist transmits healthy, vital fluid—by using magnetic stroking or the laying on of hands—directly into the nervous system of the sick person. Through his will he is also able to stimulate the patient's own will, and in this way liberates the healing forces present in the patient's body. In the same way he is also able to affect the diseased substances and drain them away from the body.

During hypnosis, the patient is put into a trance, or hypnotic sleep, as it is also called. In hypnosis the patient relinquishes his will power and his individuality. On the other hand, in treatment with healing magnetism, the patient retains consciousness and will power. Another reason why these therapies are not really comparable is the fact that their application in certain illnesses—both in hypnosis and in healing magnetism—is very different, especially as far as the cause of illness is concerned.

Both therapies have their own merit. It is even possible to use both methods of treatment in conjunction if this seems to be necessary. For instance, during a session of healing magnetism, it is possible to transfer new life force to a person in poor physical health while the psyche can be treated with hypnosis in another session.

In this context it should be pointed out that obviously all other medicinal and physical therapies can be continued during a magnetic cure. There is no need to stop any prescribed medicines, baths, or physiotherapy.

Two main types of magnetic therapy can be distinguished. The first type uses the magnetic field created by natural or artificial magnets. Since nowadays it is possible to produce artificial permanent magnets with a comparatively strong magnetic field, natural magnets made from the magnetic stone (magnetic iron or lodestone), are very rarely found on the market. Moreover, the advantage of using artificial permanent magnets is that it is possible to supply them with a considerably stronger magnetic field than the magnets found in nature. These healing magnets, bio-magnets, or whatever you wish to call them, are produced in the form of discs, sheets and sticks of different sizes and weights, and consequently with magnetic fields of varying strength.

There are various possible applications of these magnets: there are the pea-sized permanent magnets, which are on the market in the form of magnet plasters. These are small (round or square) plasters with the magnet in the center. The plaster is put on the most suitable acupuncture points and is left there for some time (a maximum of six days, depending on the reaction of the skin). Since the magnets used for the plaster are produced in vast quantities, and are therefore quite cheap, they do not need to be used again and a new magnet plaster can be used every time. As the actual magnet is so small, it only has a weak magnetic field (on average, 500 gauss).

Larger and thicker permanent magnets are rather different. These are more expensive, but they have the advantage that they keep indefinitely and can be used again and again. These magnets can be placed on the sick part of the body, sewn into the clothes, worn round the neck, or tied on. They are especially suitable for people with sensitive skin who cannot tolerate plasters. Since they have a considerably strong magnetic field (about 1000 gauss), they have a powerful effect. Moreover, it is possible to wear several magnets at the same time.

In the case of magnetic field therapy the magnetic force needed for treatment is produced by electricity. There are several instruments for this purpose. The best known is probably the magnetic cylinder. This is a hollow spool, with a diameter of 19 inches, and is about 19 inches in length. The patient is put into this cylinder or the cylinder is put upside down over the patient, who is in a sitting position.

With the latest instruments, the magnetic field is radiated, not as a continuous force field, but at set intervals which can be regulated by means of the appropriate wiring. Over the years the best results have been found to be produced by using frequencies of around 10 Hertz. In medicine this is referred to as "a large scale pulsating magnetic field," a treatment with "a low frequency pulsating electromagnetic field in the ELF region (ELF = Extremely Low Frequency)."

The magnetic lines of force completely penetrate the parts of the body exposed to them and react with the sodium and potassium ions which are of great importance as the carriers of electrical charges for all the functions of cells. By means of magnetic field therapy the electrical potential between the cells is changed. The consequence of this is a higher ionic exchange. This procedure, referred to as ion dynamics, corrects the frequently deficient processing of oxygen by the cells and produces the therapeutic benefits of the magnetic field.

The main areas of application are: inflammatory and degenerative diseases of the abdomen and the limbs, bone fractures, sporting injuries, neuralgia and metabolic disorders. The large scale, pulsating magnetic field is also used to speed up the healing of wounds.

Magnetic therapy and magnetic field therapy have nothing in common with healing magnetism for the healing magnetism that we will learn here teaches us to use an energy transmitted from our hands. No exterior tools are needed.

HISTORY OF MAGNETISM

Before we proceed into the practical application of healing magnetism, it is important for students to understand the background of this ancient healing art. We will not delve so deeply into the history as to bore students, but it is important that you are somewhat familiar with the role of the Egyptians and Greeks, as well as the role of laying-on-of-hands healing mentioned in the Bible. Also, students should be familiar with Paracelsus, Franz Mesmer, Mesmer's famous theories, and Carl von Reichenbach and his Od theory.

The Egyptians

As long ago as 3000 B.C., the Egyptian culture was flourishing. Evidence of their incomparable architecture has survived into modern times. Although a great deal of research has been carried out into the nature and culture of the ancient Egyptians, many aspects of this civilization still remain a mystery to scholars and archeologists. However, new discoveries are made every day and further mysteries are unveiled.

A civilization that had achieved such a high standard of culture must necessarily have possessed outstanding medical knowledge.

This was certainly the case, as is confirmed by the pictures in the surviving temples, buildings and funeral chambers, as well as by the ancient scripts that have been discovered and handed down.

In 1860, an American, Edwin Smith, acquired a papyrus scroll which had originally been discovered in the temple field of Thebes (Karnak). The manuscript was called "the Smith papyrus," after its new owner. In 1930, amazing revelations were published from this manuscript, which led to the conclusion that the Smith papyrus was, in fact, one of the oldest medical textbooks.

The "Ebers papyrus" gained a similar reputation. This was named after professor Georg Ebers (1837-1898), who published his translation of a papyrus scroll in Leipzig in 1875. At the time the scroll was described as a "hermetically sealed book on the Egyptian theory of medicine."

Both papyri had been written between the 19th and the 16th century B.C. However, today we know that these papyri are copies of documents dating back to the 28th century B.C., i.e., to the time of Imhotep. These two papyri are not the only scrolls that confirm the

Figure 2. An ancient Egyptian representation of resuscitation from the dead by means of magnetism.

existence of a great medical body of knowledge in the time of ancient Egypt. The Kahun papyrus (named after the place where it was discovered) refers to medical knowledge and practices that can be compared with our own. In ancient Egypt the healing skill was practiced by both physicians and priests. Some healers were even worshipped as deities.

It seems strange to us that even in those days there were specialists. There were opticians, gynecologists, general practitioners, dentists, veterinary surgeons and priest physicians, all of whom possessed astonishing diagnostic and therapeutic skills. There was a special title for the "physician for unknown illnesses"—it is possible that this title referred to healing magnetism. There were even consultants. The hieroglyphs found on a tombstone dating from around 2700 B.C. tell of a doctor named Hesire, who was called "Royal scribe, Master of physicians and dentists," which is roughly the equivalent of a consultant.

As there was such a high standard of medical knowledge, it is hardly surprising that healing magnetism was already known in ancient Egypt. In the Ebers papyrus it says: "Lay your hand on him to ease his pain and order his suffering to disappear." The goddess, Muth, said to Ramses III: "Stretch out both my arms so as to perform the SA strokes at the back of your head." It is reported that the physician, Thotembi, cured Ramses XII's sister-in-law, Princess Bentrosh of Mesopotamia, using magnetic treatment. This physician was also called "Master of his Will and Master of his Fingers." This clearly indicates that he was a magnetopath.

In order to be able to practice magnetic healing, healing temples were built. The best known is probably the temple of Imhotep in Saqqarah. This temple was famous for miracle cures (see figure 2). For more than two thousand years the sick came from Upper and Lower Egypt to be treated there. In the Nile delta and as far as the region around Thebes, there were many more healing temples named after Imhotep. Imhotep (Greek: Imuthes) was regarded as the God of the physicians; even two thousand years after his death, the Greeks valued him as highly as their own healing god, Aesculapius. Temples to Imhotep were built in Greece.

The Egyptian doctors were highly esteemed, not only in their own country, but in the surrounding states as well. In those days it was fashionable at foreign courts to have one's own Egyptian physician, or to travel to Egypt to be treated there.

It is interesting to note that Egyptian physicians were already using holistic medicine and had a strict code of professional ethics. The ancient textbooks repeatedly exhort the physicians to be "sympathetic towards their sick and never to give up a patient...." The physicians knew the limitations of their skill, for all physicians were obliged to inform the patient when they were unable to treat a disease.

During the course of history nearly all the healing temples were destroyed. What remained (until about 300 A.D.) of the old capital of Memphis was later destroyed by the Islamic conquerors. They built mosques and palaces for themselves from the remains of the temples and pyramids. The city walls of Cairo were also built from these stones at a later date. Memphis, the former center of Imhotep, is now only an insignificant ruined place on the lower Nile above Cairo, with no more than the ruined remains of the temple surviving.

The Bible

The Bible contains numerous examples and records of magnetic healing processes and activities. The Old Testament tells a story of King David, who, when he was an old man, was unable to get warm, even when covered with clothes. Therefore a young healthy girl was sought to warm up the king, and with whom he should "sleep himself back to health." The choice fell upon the fair and strong Abisag from Shuna in Israel, who cherished the king and ministered to him (I Kings 1: 1-4). Because of this the concept of sleeping with someone to bring them back to health was called Shunomatism. This method of youth or health sleeping was frequently mentioned in medical works. There is, for instance, the story of the aged English Lady Bath, who had the good health of two girls transferred to her, causing the two "donors of fluid" to become ill. According to the "law of communicating vessels," the current flows over to the weaker, older, sick partner.

In the Gospel according to St. Matthew, there is a story—apart from the other healings which Jesus carried out—about two blind men who implored him to restore their eyesight. Jesus touched their eyes and they saw. He impressed on them not to tell anyone about the healings, but they did not obey. This resulted in more and more sick people being brought to him (St. Matthew 9: 27-31).

The Gospel according to St. Luke tells of a deformed woman who had not been able to straighten up for eighteen years. When Christ saw her, he called her to him, laid his hands on her, and liberated her from her illness (St.Luke 13: 11-13).

Not only Jesus Christ, but also his disciples, who should really be called his pupils, were able to accompish healing. In a letter to Timothy, the apostle Paul advises him: "Neglect not the gift that is in thee, which was given thee by prophecy, with the laying on of the hands of the presbytery. Meditate on these things; give thyself wholly to them that thy profiting may appear to all (Timothy 4: 14-15)." On the island of Malta, Publius' father, the ruler of the island, was taken ill with a fever and dysentery. Paul went to see him, prayed, laid his hands on him and healed him (Acts of the Apostles 28:8).

If one tried to explain the numerous healings which Jesus Christ and his disciples accomplished, without resorting to polemical arguments, one would undoubtedly come to the conclusion that they reveal a strong "odic" transference of energy. In any case Reichenbach's od theory (which we shall discuss later in Part 1) confirms most of the biblical miracles.

As a result of their natural way of life and their high ethical standards, Jesus Christ and his disciples, pupils, and successors were able to radiate the fluids at an extremely powerful and intense level. By the mere laying on of hands, breathing upon a patient, and even with a glance, they were able to transmit large quantities of strong, healthy fluid energy to the sick. This was reinforced by a concentration of the will to heal. The balance of the disturbed od proportions was thus immediately reestablished and the sick person would feel better immediately and consider himself to be healed.

Since, from a modern point of view, the Bible does not give us a precise diagnosis of the illnesses Jesus and his disciples cured, but merely the symptoms from which the sick suffered, we must assume that the cases concerned were not of a traumatic or incurable nature. Nevertheless, there is no doubt that the transference of the od force, vital magnetism, fluid energy or whatever name is used for this elemental force, can lead to an improvement, even in desperate cases—if only temporarily.

This much seems to be certain: in Christ's lifetime healing magnetism again played an important part in the curing of diseases of all kinds. According to the Savior, as he stated before his Ascension, a time will come when "they shall lay hands on the sick and they shall recover" (St. Mark 16: 18).

The Greeks

Since the physicians in ancient Greece had, to a large extent, learned their skills from the Egyptians, it goes without saying that they were acquainted with magnetic healing and with the practical applications of healing magnetism. In 525 B.C. King Kambyses (died 522 B.C.), king of the Persians and the Medes, subjugated Egypt and Libya three years before his death, bringing the culturally advanced kingdom of the Pharoahs under his dominion.

Figure 3. Hippocrates (460-377 B.C.)

During the war which resulted in the subjugation of Egypt, a large number of healing temples and medical centers were destroyed. One of these was the famous medical academy of Sais, situated in the Nile delta. The tradition of this academy was continued later on by the famous medical school in Alexandria. Archimedes (287-212 B.C.), the most important mathematician and physicist of antiquity, to whom we still owe important inventions and discoveries, studied there. The Greek geographer, Strabon (c. 63 B.C.–26 A.D.), wrote that the famous Greek philosophers, Plato and Euxodus, had studied in Egypt under the priests for about thirteen years.

Thus it is certain that the Greeks, and not only their physicians, were familiar with vital magnetism and its application as a healing force. According to Solon's aphorisms, collected by Stobaios, a Greek writer of the fifth century A.D.: "Great suffering often results from slight pain, and soothing remedies are given in vain; but he who is tortured by a terrible malignant illness can suddenly be cured by the laying on of hands."

Hippocrates, the most famous physician of antiquity, is sometimes regarded as the father of medicine. He was familiar with healing magnetism and included it in his theories. (See figure 3.) In his time, Hippocrates followed the two fundamental foundations of medicine, the scientific school of medicine and the science of nature cures, as equivalent methods of treatment. He made a clear distinction between diagnosis and therapy, and for the first time took into account the patient's constitution. He drew up firm rules and regulations regarding the relationship of the physician and his patients, and recognized that the physician also had to be a psychotherapist. Hippocrates called magnetism "the force which flows from many people's hands."

Four hundred years later, the Roman, Pliny the Elder (23-79 A.D.), wrote the following words in *Naturalis Historia* (Natural History), in which he was the first to present all the natural phenomena in encyclopedic form and in a deliberate order: "There are people whose bodies contain medicinal powers."

A hundred and fifty years later, Galen (129-199 A.D.), one of the great figures of medical history, physician to the Emperor Marcus Aurelius and author of numerous works, which, together with Hippocrates' writings, were leading works in this field until the Middle Ages, thought that "a sick body can gain strength from the unbroken contact with a healthy body."

Paracelsus

Theophrastus Philippus Bombastus von Hehenheim, known as Paracelsus, is recognized as the most famous physician of the Middle Ages, despite all the hostility and intolerance with which he was viewed during his lifetime, and to some extent even today, despite all the attempts to suppress and ridicule his work. (See figure 4.) His work and records still act as inspiration for open-minded doctors today. Alternative medicine, especially the science of natural healing, is hardly conceivable in its contemporary form without Paracelsus' body of knowledge.

Paracelsus was born on November 11, 1493 in a farmhouse in Etzel, near the Devil's bridge over the River Sihl, not far from Einsiedeln in Switzerland. His father, Wilhelm Bombast von Hohenheim, was a physician and originated from Swabia. We do not know where Hohenheim studied and graduated. From a close study of the sources it seems certain that he moved from Villach in Corinthia, where his father had moved in 1502 to work as a physi-

Figure 4. Paracelsus (1493-1541)

cian and chemist, to the Italian town of Ferrera. His aim was to matriculate at the university there as a student of medicine.

However, the young natural scientist was not satisfied with the way in which the university was run. He travelled the world in search of experience in the treatment of illnesses, and explored the wonderful works of nature. In the autumn of 1526 he was appointed at the University of Basle as municipal physician and lecturer in the science of healing. He was extremely popular there because he lectured in German, which was unheard of in those days.

His good relationship with the people, and above all, his heal-ing successes, which occasionally bordered on the miraculous, earned him the envy of many people, particularly the orthodox doctors whose nonsensical healing methods he repeatedly con-demned, and which, he claimed, actually harmed patients. His view that "the study of medicine alone is by no means enough to make a good physician," brought him into conflict with the prejudices of his contemporary scholars. His disagreements with the physicians and scientists of orthodox medicine reached such a pitch that Paracelsus had to flee by night from Basle to Strasbourg.

Paracelsus worked as a physician, natural scientist, philoso-pher and theologian when the arts and sciences were flourishing. His contemporaries included Albrecht Durer, Copernicus, Zwingli, Hans Sachs, the Hapsburg Emperor Charles V, Leonardo da Vinci, both Hans Holbein the Elder and Hans Holbein the Younger, Michelangelo, Raphael, Titian, Tilman Riemenscheider, Lucas Cra-nach, Mathias Grunewald and other great figures in the history of civilization. Famous personalities like Ulrich from Hutten and Eras-mus from Rotterdam were amongst his patients.

When considering a scientist and a scholar such as Paracelsus, one may assume as a matter of course that he was already ahead of his time in being concerned with magnetism and its application for the purposes of healing. Paracelsus actually stated that the earth was a huge magnet, and that all living creatures on earth were influenced by this natural magnetism. He was familiar with the practice of healing magnetism and with the transference of vital forces. A precise description of this phenomenon can be found in his work *De Origine Morborum Invisibulum.*

He was also concerned with polarity and the fact that opposites attract each other. He called healing based on this method "sym-pathetic cures." His starting point was that all like things attract opposite forces. According to this view, illness can be eliminated by transferring the ill substances to another person, plant or animal. If this is done taking certain precautions, the ill substances are, as it were, "sucked out" of the body.

Paracelsus termed the vital force *mumia* and supposed that it led to the removal of the illness. When one removes the ill substances, they adhere to the mumia. He called these substances containing the mumia magnets, because they attract the illness when they are transferred to another living being, or are buried or destroyed in any way. (In the case of healing magnetism as we know it, the mumia can be destroyed by shaking it off, or it can be destroyed under running water.)

Paracelsus divided illnesses into five categories, according to their causes:

1. Illnesses which have their cause in the astral body and in astral influences (Ens Astrale).

2. Illnesses which result from pollution and poisonous substances (Ens Vale).

3. Illnesses which arise from individual characteristics (Ens Naturale).

4. Illnesses which are produced by magic influences (Ens Spirituale).

5. Illness produced by the effect of God's law (Karma).

From these distinctions between the causes of illness it is easy to recognize that Paracelsus' thinking was based on the concept of a vital fluid, the true elemental force.

According to Paracelsus, there are no medicines for the treatment of illness, but only healing forces, which, if administered in the correct dosage at the correct moment, make it possible for the sick person to heal himself. Theophrastus von Hohenheim also recognized that the healing could be mobilized by transferring the vital energy lacking in a particular organism to the weakened organism.

Paracelsus can be described as the greatest physician of the Middle Ages with complete justification, but he died in Salzburg in 1541, impoverished and abandoned. He once said: "The highest level of medicine is love." Anyone who has made a careful study of the life and work of this great natural scientist and philosopher knows that he was talking of the deep love that exists between people. The manifestation of the practitioner's wish to help the patient has always played an important part in natural healing.

Franz Anton Mesmer

On May 23, 1734, Ventor Anton Mesmer, from Iznang on Lake Constance, forest warden and hunter to the Prince Bishop of Constance, entered the birth of his third child in the baptismal register of Weiler, a nearby parish. The parents of Franz Anton Mesmer were descended from an old family. The grandfather, Johannes Mesmer (1677-1747), had been master of the hunt in the episcopal service at Wollmatingen near Constance.

The future doctor, Franz Anton Mesmer, spent his childhood at Lake Constance. The deep woods, fertile meadows and waterland, the Rhine and the lake itself, the dominating peaks of the Swiss mountains on the horizon, all shaped Mesmer's youth and developed in him a close relation with nature. From this closeness with the marvelous world around him grew the urge to discover the mysteries of nature, to understand them and dominate them. (See figure 5 on page 22.)

At age eight Mesmer attended the village school, where his intelligence aroused the priests' special interest. He was sent to a nearby monastery (presumably to the Franciscans) where he was to learn music and Latin. As a twelve-year-old he attended the Jesuit college at Constance, which he left at sixteen. His entry to the college (which was an outstanding episcopal school of the time) was considered a great honor for the village child.

His achievements there paved the way for the best course of education known at the time: he was able to attend the Jesuit university at Dillingen, in Bavarian Swabia, with a scholarship from the Bishop. After this he studied at the Bavarian University of

Figure 5. Franz Anton Mesmer (1734-1815)

Ingolstadt; his matriculation there was recorded on November 3, 1754. Five years later he was at the University of Vienna, where he dedicated himself to the study of medicine. This decision was certainly influenced by the fact that this distinguished medical educational institution offered the best medical training.

On May 27, 1776 the then thirty-two year old Mesmer graduated as a doctor of medicine. His thesis, entitled "De planetarium influxu (On the Influence of the Planets)," was to form the basis of his life's work. This physical-medical doctoral thesis deals with the influence of the stars upon the human body. Mesmer described an unknown force which "penetrates the deepest core of any matter, pouring out from the infinite celestial space," and therefore affects our bodies.

Initially Vienna proved to be a lucky town for Mesmer: on January 10, 1768, "the nobly born and highly educated Master Anton Mesmer, medical doctor, bachelor, born in Moersburg in Swabia, was married to Maria Anna von Posch, a lady of noble birth" in St. Stephen's church in Vienna. The young couple moved

Figure 6. Mesmer in Paris. (Source: Musée Carnavalet)

into the splendid house which was a wedding present from his wife, and Mesmer built a laboratory and had his practice there. He had a passion for music, and many artists were guests in his home, including both Mozarts, the father and the son.

In 1777 he took over the treatment of Miss Paradis, an eighteen year old talented pianist, who had gone blind at thirteen. The most famous doctors of the day had tried to treat the girl, but all declared her incurable. When Mesmer reported that he had succeeded in healing her, a public scandal broke out because the doctors—who had originally confirmed the healing—later declared the whole thing to be a fraud. There is no doubt that Mesmer was right, and it seems likely that the girl became blind again as a result of all the excitement and turmoil of her daily life in the family circle.

However, Mesmer had had enough of Vienna and of the intrigues against him by envious colleagues. He was convinced of the truth of the old adage that "the prophet is never recognized in his own country," and moved to Munich. However, he did not stay there long and by 1778 he moved to Paris. (See figure 6.) At first

Mesmer had not intended to start a practice in Paris, but had merely wanted a break. However, as his reputation had preceded him there, doctors and scholars soon tried to contact him.

Convinced of his subject, Mesmer now took every opportunity to make healing magnetism a matter of public knowledge in France as well, and he soon had a large and flourishing practice. Eminent people from the most distinguished circles sought his acquaintance and wished to be treated by him. The prominent figures of Paris thronged to his salon in order to be magnetized by the master. He gained widespread popularity and even the Queen, Marie Antoinette, noticed him after he healed one of her ladies-in-waiting.

At first his critics and enemies remained silent, but soon the envy broke out again and Mesmer was exposed, as before, to slander and ridicule. (See figure 7.) Finally his opponents set up an investigating committee, the members of which were largely orthodox doctors and Mesmer's opponents, which undertook to discover the "truth" about his theories. Mesmer repeatedly explained that his new healing method could not possibly be analyzed objectively by

Figure 7. Caricature of magnetism, 19th century. (Source: National Library, Estampes)

the medical doctrine of the time. Animal magnetism was no secret device, as the medical profession imagined, but rather a science with its own causes, consequences and laws. Mesmer explained categorically that he had no need of judges, but pupils. His theories and his system were discussed before the Medical Academy in a public session. These discussions degenerated into chaos, and finally his thesis and system were rejected.

He suffered the same fate as many other pioneers of the healing art; although the representatives of orthodox medicine denied that healing magnetism had any effect, and argued that it did not exist, or dismissed proven healing successes as fraud, in the same breath they warned against the risks involved in this new method of healing. In a secret report, the contents of which were to be withheld from the public, the members of the committee warned the government to continue to keep an eye on the new healing method because this (nonexistent) magnetism was dangerous and harmful. The authors of such claims did not seem in the least disturbed that in this way they were making a mockery of their own strongly represented ideas. Yet it is perfectly logical that if something does not exist, it cannot have any effect. Similarly, a form of medicine which is denied to have any effect cannot be harmful.

Although Mesmer's friends began collecting signatures for a large petition throughout France to encourage him to remain in Paris, he nevertheless returned to Germany. He had written several books in Paris describing his theories and experiences with animal magnetism. In 1779, his report "Memoire sur la Decouverte du Magnetisme Animal (Report on the Discovery of Animal Magnetism)" was published. This work contains the twenty-seven theses which are now referred to as the basis of healing magnetism. By 1781 a book appeared in French, entitled *A Short History of Animal Magnetism up to April 1781*.

On March 15, 1815, Doctor Mesmer died (at the age of eighty-one) from a stroke in his Swabian home of Meersburg on Lake Constance. His funeral was a very solemn affair, and a large crowd of mourners gathered, for Mesmer had always been a benefactor of the poor and sick and was highly esteemed by all those who knew him closely.

In 1830, fifteen years after his death, the Berlin Society of Natural Scientists had a monument erected in the cemetery in Meersburg, where Mesmer was buried, in recognition of his

Figure 8. Mesmer's tomb in the churchyard at Meersburg, on Lake Constance. (Photograph: Hagemann)

achievements in the natural sciences. (See figure 8.) It is still possible to visit this memorial stone in the cemetery of Meersburg, close to the chapel on the west wall. A triangular block of marble rises from a sandstone slab resembling an altar. Originally there was a sundial and a compass on the top, protected by a small dome-shaped roof.

Just as Mesmer's work and doctrine were disputed in his own lifetime, his work and legacy still (one hundred and seventy years after his death) form a favorite target for many orthodox doctors, as well as teachers and sympathizers who follow their example, even today. As they do not understand healing magnetism, and generally do not even want to understand it, they use it as one of the many excuses to argue against the natural healing methods. So be it. We will content ourselves with a quotation by Alec Mellor, dating from 1958: "The day will come, and it will be a big day, when Mesmer will be posthumously recognized, as is only to be expected. Few people will deny that they discovered valuable concepts in his work, to put it simply, and not only healers will hold this view."

Mesmer's theories

By the concept of magnetism, Mesmer meant a fluid pervading the the entire universe, through the movements of which one animal body can have an effect upon another. These movements he called animal magnetism.

According to Mesmer, health consists of a state of harmony. Consequently, illness is a state in which harmony, (i.e., the trouble-free interaction of all somatic and psychological functions) is disturbed. Since there is only one harmony, there is only one state of health. This was by no means a new idea, as Paracelsus had repeatedly expressed the same point of view in his work.

In our day the definition of the word health does not differ much from Mesmer's theory: The World Health Organization (WHO) defines the concept of health as a state of the "complete physical, psychological and social well-being." One of the fundamental human rights is the right to the best possible health. This condition cannot easily be reduced to a simple formula, since every person is an individual and different from everyone else. Good health results from the sum of a person's physical, spiritual, and mental attitudes and proper somatic functioning. In his work, *Report on the Discovery of Animal Magnetism*, Mesmer put forward twenty-seven theories which, in a figurative sense, still apply up to this day, particularly his discourse on polarity and fluid. Briefly, they are as follows:

1. There is a mutual influence of celestial bodies, the earth and living bodies.

2. The medium for this influence is a universally present and continuous fluid, which permeates everywhere. It is fine beyond comparison, and by its nature, is capable of receiving, spreading and communicating all influences of movement.

3. The mutual influence is subject to laws of mechanics which are as yet unknown.

4. Alternative effects can result from this influence, which can be considered as influx and reflux.

5. The influx and reflux can be more or less general, more or less individual, and more or less coincidental.

6. Through the most universal process of nature, active connections are established between the celestial bodies, the earth and its component parts.

7. The properties of matter and of organic bodies depend on this process.

8. The living body feels the alternative effects of this fluid: by penetrating the nerves, these are directly affected.

9. Characteristics comparable to a magnet manifest themselves particularly in the human body. Different opposite poles which can be linked, changed, destroyed or strengthened can be distinguished; even the phenomenon of diffraction can be observed here.

10. The characteristic of the living body which renders it receptive to the influence of the celestial bodies and their mutual effects surrounding it, and which becomes clear through the similarity with the magnet, has induced me to call it "animal magnetism."

11. The influence and the force of animal magnetism described above can be transferred to other living or non-living bodies. Both are more or less receptive.

12. The effect and the force can be increased and can be spread through the same bodies.

13. In attempting to do this, one notices a flowing out of matter which penetrates all bodies, without losing any of its influence.

14. It can have an effect over long distances without the help of any intermediate body.

15. It can be enlarged or reflected, as light is enlarged or reflected by a mirror.

16. It is transmitted, spread and increased by sound.

17. The magnetic force can be accumulated, concentrated and transported.

18. I have stated that not all living bodies are receptive in the same way. There are even bodies which have a resistance so that their mere existence cancels the effects of magnetism in other bodies— although this is very rare.

19. Moreover, this resistance penetrates all bodies. It can be conveyed, strengthened, concentrated and transmitted by sound. It is not very detrimental; on the contrary, it is an opposite positive force.

20. The natural and artificial magnet may contain the force of an animal magnetism and its positive force, without any change in its effect on the compass. Consequently the principle of magnetism differs from that of the minerals.

21. This system provides new insights into the nature of fire and light, as well as into the theory of attraction, influx and reflux, magnetism and electricity.

22. It becomes clear that with regard to illness, the magnet and artificial electricity only have qualities which are also characteristic of many other factors. When their application has a positive effect, this is based on animal magnetism.

23. From the practical rules I have established, it is clear that this principle can heal mental illness directly, and all other illness indirectly.

24. With its help, the use of medicines becomes clear to the doctor; he has to perfect their effect and has to create and lead curative crises.

25. By expounding my method, with the help of a new theory of illness, I illustrate the universal unity of the principle.

26. With the help of this knowledge, the doctor will safely recognize the nature and development of even the most complicated illnesses. He can thus prevent a deterioration without exposing the sick person to to dangerous effects or detrimental consequences, regardless of the patient's age, temperament, or sex. Women can benefit from these advantages during pregnancy and in childbirth.

27. This doctrine helps the doctor judge the state of health of any person and to protect him from illnesses to which he might be exposed. The healing art has thus achieved the highest degree of perfection.

• • •

The thesis can easily be summarized as follows (as shown by Tenhaeff):

1. There is a connecting force which penetrates the whole universe; a perfect, movable and incomparably fine substance.

2. All illness results from the fact that disturbances in the balance of this force develop in the body of the person affected by illness (an unharmonious distribution of the force in the body).

3. Healing consists of reestablishing the balance.

4. The restoration of the balance has to result from the supply of this mysterious force to the body of the sick person.

5. The force should be supplied by a magnetizer-doctor. He should be familiar not only with medical teaching, but also with the technique of magnetizing and the possibilities available to him of receiving radiation of the substance which he has to transmit to his patient, to let it flow through him to increase or decrease the strength before transmitting the required amount to the patient.

6. The magnetizer has to know how he can transmit his force to different patients in the most effective way.

Mesmer's main achievement undoubtedly lies in the fact that he taught the methodical application of certain movements of the hands in a way that had been unknown up to then. The essential features of his theory and his method have proved so successful in practice that up to the time of writing, very few improvements have been made.

The view that Mesmer was the sole discoverer of healing magnetism is based above all on Wolfart's work. In 1815, Wolfart published a two volume work on Mesmerism in Berlin. Nowadays, however, it is generally agreed that Mesmer merely extended this form of therapy. He was inspired by the writings of Paracelsus, van Helmont, Goclenius, Burggravis, Widrig, Kircher, Santanelli and Maxwell.

A lecture by the French psychologist and psychiatrist, Dr. Paul Farez, given in September, 1902 to the Parisian Society of Hypnosis and Psychology, can be considered as one proof of this view. With the help of quotations from the works of the above-mentioned scientists, Farez showed that Mesmer's writings on magnetic fluid contained many ideas taken from the above authors, which he repeated virtually verbatim. Nevertheless, Franz Anton Mesmer deserves to be called the founder of modern fluid therapy and healing magnetism.

Carl von Reichenbach and the Od Theory

Since the discovery of animal magnetism by Mesmer there have been many attempts to prove the existence of this new and still unknown force experimentally. Carl Freiherr von Reichenbach was the first to provide the physical basis for this. Reichenbach, a doctor of philosophy, was born in Stuttgart on February 12, 1788, and was, like Mesmer, of Swabian descent. (See figure 9.) In his time, Reichenbach was a well-known industrialist, an astute natural scientist, and above all, an excellent chemist. His name will not be forgotten in the history of chemistry, for he discovered creosote and paraffin. (Creosote is a distillation produced from beechwood tar,

Figure 9. Carl Freiherr von Reichenbach. (An oil painting by Ludivike Simanowitz. The original hangs in the Justinus-Kerner-Haus, Weinsberg. Used by permission of the Justinus-Kerner-Vereins, Weinsberg Wuertt.)

and was formerly used as a disinfectant; paraffin is used in the chemical industry for making candles and ointments as an insulation and preserving agent.) In addition, he gained great acclaim from his theory of meteorites, of which he himself had a large collection. He also made a name for himself in speleology. However, Baron von Reichenbach achieved his true fame from the discovery of an astral substance which he called "Od" or Od magnetic force, after the Nordic god, Odin (from the Icelandic *Odr*, i.e., force). This subtle fluid is the generating force of all those physiological manifestations called vital magnetism.

The discovery of Od and his work, experiments, and publications on this subject did not bring him only recognition. On the one hand, he was valued and respected as a precise natural scientist, above all as a chemist and botanist who had discovered important new substances, and his achievements in cave exploration as well as in meteorites were universally honored. He was also publically attacked for his Od theory during his lifetime.

Reichenbach lived almost half his life in a country house in Kobenzl, near Vienna, in the small castle of Reisenberg. The old Baron had the reputation of being a magician, the visionary of Kobenzl with the people of Vienna. It was rumored that in the basement of his small country castle he had a pitch black room, where he allowed no light to enter. He had another chamber built into this room, so it must have been hellish dark in there. The old man pursued his black and visionary skills in this dark chamber. Even after his death, the Baron was regarded by the people of Vienna as a cranky eccentric.

What was the truth of all this, and what was mere fantasy? What kind of man was Freiherr von Reichenbach really? In his introduction to Reichenbach's book on Od magnetism (1921 edition), Dr. Friederich Feerhow writes this about the author: "In reality Reichenbach offered enlightenment rather than mysticism, as his attitude to animal magnetism, and especially to spiritualism, clearly shows. He was a man who enjoyed life, was urged on by a clear drive which raised him to the ranks of the nobility, and was genuinely in pursuit of knowledge, an ideal contemporary representative of the natural sciences. His technical achievements, his chemical and geological discoveries bear witness to his sober approach and keen intelligence; and when one takes into account Reichenbach's contributions towards the body of scientific knowledge and his pioneering role in industry, it is impossible to reject an entire, extensive branch of his research as being strange, for the same able mind produced and researched this branch of science, and passionately insisted on the importance of the science of "Od."...

How did Reichenbach come to research a scientific field that was absolutely new territory for him as a chemist? What stimulated him to carry out research in a field that was completely alien to him? One day a Viennese doctor, Doctor Eisenstein, asked Reichenbach's opinion about a confusing case: one of his patients described a curious influence that he felt when he was close to a magnet. In addition, he thought he could perceive manifestations of light in the dark which other people could not see. Reichenbach checked the man's statement with the help of a strong magnet and confirmed the claim.

This event provided the impetus for an endless series of studies. After numerous experiments carried out in a strictly scientific manner, Reichenbach showed that a brightness which wraps the whole body and which is visible and perceptible under certain circumstances, emanates from the human body. This emanation or fluid he described as "cosmic dynamite," and he named it after the old German concept of the all-pervading god, Odin, Od.

Reichenbach published his first experiments in a series of treatises. His work, *Examinations of the Dynamide*, was published in 1849. Between 1854 and 1855 he wrote his great work, *A Sensitive Person's Attitude to Od*. In this standard work he discussed various sensations which sensitive people feel under the influence of Od force in certain conditions. In addition to the phenomenon of Od light, Reichenbach was able to influence the whole body or parts of the body by stroking with the hands, though without actually touching the person in question. (The earlier magnetizers referred to this stroking as making passes. Nowadays we call it magnetic stroking.)

Reichenbach discovered that by using downward strokes in the direction from the head to the feet, following the course of the nerves, he could provoke cool and pleasant sensations in the form of a feeling of peace, a need for sleep and relaxation. When the strokes were used the other way round, i.e., from the feet to the head, this caused excitement and the need for sleep disappeared, while a feeling of warmth spread throughout the body. This confirms the magnetism which had been used for healing purposes.

Having considered all the research, the Od can be described as the material carrier of the vital force, because healthy Od can be transmitted to a sick organism and have a healing effect. It does not lose its effect when it is transferred to another body. Od is also the carrier of thoughts, as proved by telepathy. To summarize: Od is the vital fluid which prevails throughout nature. Owing to its fine material quality, it penetrates all coarse materials, especially wood, metals and organic substances.

Reichenbach's fundamental belief that everything radiates is confirmed with certainty by the latest results in research, and his work can be described as one of the greatest achievements of the higher fields of knowledge. He died on January 19, 1859, in Leipzig. Future scientists who are concerned with vital fluid will not be able to ignore his work.

Od radiation in human beings

According to Reichenbach's discoveries, Od radiates from all organic and non-organic bodies. In fact, the entire universe seems to be filled with it. The human organism produces this vital fluid all the time and emits it continuously. A continuous cycle of fine, magnetic substance takes place, determined by the chemical and physical processes which are constantly taking place in the human body.

With each breath, with each movement, with each contact with objects and other people, Od can be transmitted or taken in, depending on the polarization of the person or the object concerned. Reichenbach had already proved that in the case of people, the Od is polarized. Sensitive people—about half of all people fall into this category—can easily be influenced by the radiation from the human body or from animals, plants or even mineral matter.

This emanation of fine substance is also known as an aura; to sensitive people the aura is visible, and relevant conclusions can be drawn from its shape and color, regarding the state of the fluid of the aura carrier at the time. (In medical terminology the word aura refers to a particular perception or sensation such as that clearly felt by an epileptic, usually shortly before an attack.) Insensitive people also have the potentiality, by means of appropriate exercises, as well as with aura glasses, of heightening their sensory awareness and developing a sensitivity to the oscillation of the fluid substances to such an extent that the Od rays become visible.

In order to better understand the relationships, the following question should be raised: who is sensitive? The answer was explained by Reichenbach in his Od magnetic letters. According to these letters, sensitive people have certain characteristics and features that can be easily recognized. Sensitive people:

1. Usually suffer from troubled sleep. They either sleep only for an hour at a time and then wake up, or they kick off the bedclothes and wake up because they feel cold. Many talk in their sleep.

2. Nearly always feel a dislike for everything that is yellow, and consequently for the color yellow in general, whereas blue is always experienced as a pleasant color.

3. Often shy away from looking in the mirror because they cannot bear the sight of their own reflection.

4. Always try to sit in the direction they are travelling on a bus or a train. Moreover, they will feel an urge to open the carriage window, regardless of the temperature outside or their fellow travellers.

5. Always want to sit on the last seat of the row in church, the theater, the cinema or the concert hall, so that they will be able to escape first.

6. Dislike warm, particularly overcooked dishes, greasy food and sweets. They prefer salads, simple and predominantly mildly sour dishes.

7. Cannot bear to have somebody standing behind them. They always avoid crowds, gatherings and pushing. Some find it objectionable to shake hands or to have their hand held for a while in a handshake.

8. Often feel repelled by drinking from paper cups, or eating with plastic cutlery; they cannot get to sleep lying on the left side, they are over-sensitive and irritable, they seek solitude or have a small select circle of friends.

As a consequence of their behavior and their characteristics, sensitive people are often misunderstood by their fellow men, are frequently ridiculed, considered full of ill will, and are sometimes avoided. However, people who fall in this category are particularly suitable for the purpose of experiments. They are especially able to see the Od emanations from people and animals, plants and crystals. Some are even able to feel them.

For his experiments, Reichenbach used rooms without any windows, so as to exclude the effects of light. After sensitive people stayed in absolute darkness for a while, they were able to recognize the Odic emanations and describe them accurately. The Odic aura surrounds the human body like a radiant and transparent cover which emanates to a greater or lesser extent, and shines in different colors. The entire person is surrounded by this magnetic atmosphere, which in some places glows in the form of a tail.

Reichenbach showed that polarity can be established from the color of the Odic fluid, as well as from the density and the intensity of the radiation. According to this theory, the left side of the body is Od positive, radiating in a dark bluish color, while the right side is Od negative and radiates a reddish-yellow hue.

The emanation of fluid is different in the masculine and feminine sex, and even within the same sex there is a great variation of color and shape; it is subject to certain changes, depending on the state of health. In the case of a healthy person, a strong and clear emanation can be seen, whereas in a sick person the entire Odic aura takes on a rather dirty shade of yellow.

Depending on the part and the side of the body, the human magnetic polarity is either positive or negative. The like poles repel each other, whereas the unlike poles attract each other. The body can be subdivided into different magnetic axes, so that an approximate representation of the polarity of the fluid fields can be obtained. Since each person is an individual, the emanation of the fine magnetic substance differs from person to person.

Basically one has to imagine the field of the fine magnetic substance in a three dimensional sort of way. The front left (on your right when you face another person) part of the body is positive and the front right part is negative. If one imagines a system of lines from left to right, this system would be spread over the width axis. The positive force would be strongest on the outside of the left side, and the negative force would be strongest on the right side of this half of the body. Towards the middle it becomes weaker, and the one cancels out the other. Indeed, the transition from positive to negative magnetism should not be conceived as a sudden change, but rather as a merging together of two polarities. The strongest emanation of fluid is found in the field of the width axis.

The third axis, the length axis (also called the longitudinal axis) runs down from the head to the toes and in comparison with the other two axes, is magnetically the weakest. The head is positive, the feet are negative. Following this system, the human body is a three dimensional magnetic polarity (width, depth, length). See figure 10 for a visual interpretation of this idea. Figure 11 on page 38 shows another view—the depth axis.

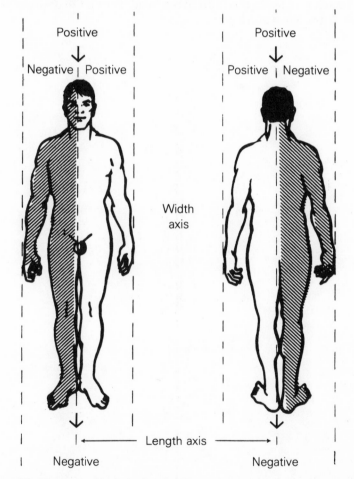

Positive

↓

Negative | Positive

Positive | Negative

Positive

↓

Positive | Negative

Width axis

Negative

←————— Length axis —————→

Negative

Figure 10. The second axis is the depth or transverse axis. It separates the body into a front and back half. Its magnetic intensity is slightly weaker. The positive pole is on the front part and the negative pole is on the back part of the body.

Apart from these three magnetic aspects of magnetism, there are extensions of the fluid substance; we will not dwell upon these here, as this would only lead to confusion, and they are not particularly important for the practice of healing magnetism as we will discuss it. During the waking state the magnetic force reveals itself most strongly in the front of the head, whereas during sleep it is strongest in the back of the head. Thus the development of the fluid forces takes place in the front of the head during the day and at the back of the head during the night.

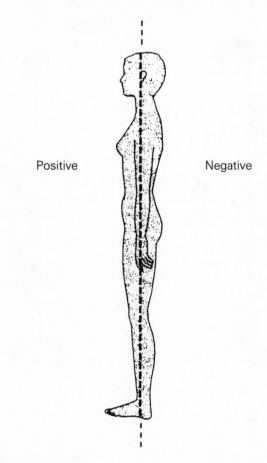

Positive   Negative

Figure 11. The depth axis.

Inside the human body the relationship of the Od poles depends very largely on the state of health. With a person in good health, the Od negativity predominates. The stronger and the more vigorous the organism, the further the polarity of the vital fluid moves to the negative side. In Reichenbach's view, extreme Odic negativity signifies an excellent state of health.

However, indisposition and illness shift the Od to the positive side. Nevertheless, the Odic manifestations differ from organism to organism in the same way that every person defines smell and taste in a different way and finds them more or less pleasant. This contrast is most noticeable between animate and inanimate matter. The tension of the Od poles which is present in the magnet, in crystal and in all living matter, dissolves when the organism dies. It disintegrates because the dead body cannot create any more Od force and is unable to attract any to it.

The Universal Aura

By about 1850 Reichenbach had proved in numerous experiments that all matter (especially highly developed organisms) has its own characteristic radiation which it emits constantly. The theory of emanation and undulation established by modern science, which endeavors to establish a scientifically precise explanation of the nature of electricity, is also based on the existence of a fine material substance. According to the theory of emanation, all matter is composed of a single element. This fine substance, also known as the mother element, can compress itself to any shape and is the fission product of electrons and ions, the smallest particles known to us.

This elemental fluid matter is constantly present in the form of an unimaginably fast spiral movement. The frequency of the coarser electrons and ions seems to be conditioned by the oscillations of this fine substance. The oscillations proceed in a spiral rotation around so–called nuclei, which are themselves in motion. It is thought that on average, these rotate at a rate of about two billion rotations per second.

The nature and substance of this elemental matter and of the nucleus are absolutely identical; the difference between the nucleus and the fine substance surrounding it depends on the different polarized directions of movement. According to the law of polarization, unlike poles attract each other and like poles repel each other. The polarization results in constant movement of the separate particles of this fine substance. Since according to the physical law of the preservation of energy there can be no loss of energy, a cycle is formed in order to maintain the balance of energy: a kind of vacuum is created wherever the fine matter has been removed, and this vacuum has the property of immediately attracting the same amount of fine matter as has been used. The balance of energy is in this way constantly maintained. Since the elemental substance can compress itself to any shape, all matter known to us consists of this primordial element. That is why we now commonly refer to this as radiating matter.

However, the sensations and perceptions of which living organisms are capable are also released through the effect of this fluid energy. Physiological processes take place in the human or animal body as a result of sensory activity, and these in turn set chemical reactions into motion. However, these reactions are not released automatically.

In order to induce a chemical process, a reaction of enzymes, a mechanical activity, a sensation relating to the nervous system, or the transformation of an idea into a picture, an effective impulse or a force is required which provides the necessary energy for all these chemical-physical processes. The five senses (sight, hearing, smell, taste and feeling) can only function by receiving fine material particles. Our nerves, and the fine substances emanating from them, have to attract or repel the fluid particles of the matter by which we are surrounded, depending on the polarization. This attraction or repulsion is described as impulses. For example, when looking at an object, the radiation from it is received by the eye (where tiny processes are taking place) and is passed on along the optic nerve to the brain; there it is processed and becomes a mental picture.

This process is, in reality, an extremely complicated interaction of various complex chemical-physical processes from the physiological field and cannot be described in more detail here. Each vital process is accomplished by means of the reception and the release of vital fluid from the universe. A surplus of fine matter is produced and is again released as a continuous emanation of fine material. Paracelsus' magnale, Mesmer's animal magnetism, Reichenbach's Od, and similar rays of later researchers (the n-rays of the physicist Blondot and the psychophysic energy of the Russian doctor Kotic) are all identical.

In the course of the history of magnetism there has been no lack of attempts to make the emanation of fine material visible and to fix it as a picture. Even Reichenbach knew that Od rays emitted from the human hand could illuminate a light-sensitive photographic plate to such an extent that the hand could easily be discerned as a formation of rays. Reichenbach performed his experiments in a dark chamber with a plate cassette which he made especially for this purpose to ensure that exposure of the plate could not be produced by outside light.

In the 1890s the Russian doctor Jacob von Narkiewicz–Jodko developed a procedure which he called electrography. Using this method he was able to photograph the emanations of nervous or vital electricity and to draw conclusions regarding the state of health of the person being examined. The Russian researcher was convinced that a healthy body emanates a stronger electric radiation than a sick or weak body. He found no emanation at all from paralyzed parts of the body.

Kirlian photography has become very popular in the last few years. It works on a similar principle and is also used for diagnostic purposes. In 1963, the Soviet couple Semjon and Valentine Kirlian patented the electro-photography which they had developed. The procedure has been used in the West since 1970 and since then the technique has been used in many fields of research—from agrarian research to dentistry.

Kirlian photography has a special use in medicine and in psychology as a good diagnostic aid, where it has proved valuable in testing stimulants. The method can also be used successfully to evaluate the discharge of corona at the end points of acupuncture, as well as for making the aura visible. Kirlian photography has also been applied in other fields as a result of the development of special instruments for the production of Kirlian photographs. The simplicity of the technique has contributed much to its widespread use because it is extremely easy and there are no problems using the Kirlian instruments.

An ordinary sheet of photographic paper (black/white or colored) is applied (in the dark room) on the working plate of the Kirlian camera, and the hand is gently placed on this. Then the instrument is switched on for a few seconds. The appliance now produces a high frequency, high voltage field which releases electric sparks between the photographic paper and the fingertips. These discharges lead to the "exposure" of the photographic emulsion.

The photographic paper then has to be developed to make the emanations of the hand visible. This is also an uncomplicated business. However, Kirlian photography is only suitable for making the Odic phenomena of the hands and feet visible, as these can easily be put onto the working plate.

Various attempts have been made to make the total aura of a person visible, i.e., the fluid emanation wrapped around the entire body. Dr. Walter J. Kilner (1847-1920), a doctor at a London hospital, was also concerned with research on making the aura visible, and wrote several essays on this subject, including his work, *The Human Atmosphere or the Aura Made Visible with the Aid of Chemical Screens*, which was published in London in 1911.[1] Kilner also created the Kilner screen, a mechanical-chemical device to make the aura visible which contains dicyanogen-blue, which was dissolved in alcohol.

Nowadays aura glasses are used to see the aura. These are special glasses fitted with lenses which let through only a certain section of the color spectrum and screen off any interfering light. Some practice and concentration is required to see the aura with these filter glasses, but success in the end makes it all worthwhile.

---

[1] This book has been reprinted by Samuel Weiser, Inc. under the title *The Aura*. The book is presently available in a paperback edition.

Part 2

MAGNETIC
THERAPY TRAINING

Every person has within himself a power which, through correct practical development, can be heightened to such an extent that he becomes able to use vital magnetic force to heal himself, as well as others, from sickness and suffering.

John Baptist Wiedenmann, 1912

WHO CAN MAGNETIZE?

Every person has the ability to transfer his own vital magnetism to another person. But this ability, like any other gift which is innate in man, is more or less pronounced in every individual. However, like any other skill, healing magnetism is subject to certain rules. Just as a painter has to be familiar with the use of color and the laws of perspective, the magnetopath must be informed about the nature of vital magnetism, anatomy and physiology of the human organism. Obviously these indispensable prerequisites also include a sound knowledge of psycho-magnetic laws and the relation of polarity. Theory and practice require constant exercise.

Anyone who wishes to practice healing magnetism frequently and perhaps professionally must, above all, be healthy himself and have a stable physical and psychic constitution. A sensible way of life and well-ordered personal relationships, sporting activities with regular breaks, sufficient sleep, regular relaxation in fresh air and nature, restraint in the consumption of food and drink are all fundamental prerequisites to preserve and increase the magnetic powers.

Magnetic healing involves transferring vital force to the patient. The practitioner therefore transfers this force in the measure that the patient receives it. The weaker the patient, the greater the loss of Od for the person treating him. Many magnetopaths report that after an effective magnetic treatment they feel completely exhausted and are only able to find the strength to carry on the treatment after stopping and resting. In this way a very weak and sick person can use up more of the magnetizer's energy in ten minutes than a less weak patient would use in half an hour of intensive treatment.

Many magnetizers agree that magnetic treatments carried out with great concentration over one or two hours require more energy than other kinds of physical work. Therapists who feel the emanation of vital force strongly from the hands are exhausted after a short time. The weakness can be especially felt in the fingers, the hands, and the arms, and it is accompanied by a feeling of emptiness and tiredness.

This can be considered as a confirmation of Reichenbach's Od theory: loss of Od is equivalent to the loss of life force. The practitioner must therefore be in good health himself before he can pass any of this vital force to another person. Sensitive people feel straightaway whether the magnetizer fulfills all the physical, mental and moral demands required to practice healing magnetism.

To what extent does the transfer of the fluid energy exhaust the person giving the treatment? The answer to this must be that it always results in a certain state of exhaustion. The transfer of physical, mental, and Odic forces causes them to be constantly regenerated. The recuperation of the human body and the resoration of its energy take place through the intake of food and oxygen, as well as through sleep, when the cells are recharged with the original element. This corresponds to the law of nature. There is no foundation for the fear that one could completely exhaust one's own vital magnetism as a result of transference.

The ability to magnetize is not related to gender. However, experience has shown that in many cases a better effect is achieved when the force is transferred to the opposite sex. This is linked to the law of cross-over in which polarity also plays a part. Therefore men achieve especially good healing results with sick and weak women, whereas female magnetizers have an extremely calming and soothing effect on men.

When people related by blood treat each other magnetically they will not be very successful. Strangely enough, this applies to brothers and sisters as well. Even male and female cousins can only in exceptional cases treat each other effectively. Here too, the relations of polarity seem to play a part. (Perhaps this is the key to the fact that blood relations only seldom live together in true harmony and that one often prefers the company of strangers rather than the constant company of blood relations.) In this context it should be mentioned that the magnetizer can never successfully treat a person whom he does not like. Similarly a patient can never hope for successful healing with a person whom he finds disagreeable.

Parents may wish to exercise a beneficial magnetic influence on their children, but the law of cross-over applies here: mothers will have a stronger magnetic effect upon their sons, and fathers upon their daughters, rather than the other way round.

It has already been emphasized that the fluid donor should be physically and mentally alert and healthy. However, this does not mean that only vigorous and energetic people can effectively practice healing magnetism. It should be pointed out that people giving treatment who are temporarily sick should only practice again when the body is completely restored and in spiritual harmony. This also applies to women during menstruation.

HOW DO YOU DO A TREATMENT?

Although the most important teachers of healing magnetism often describe different methods of treatment, this should not be a problem because they all come to the same thing in the end: the transference of vital force onto the patient. People who have long, intensive, and above all, professional experience of healing magnetism will discover that in the course of time they will develop their own style, and on the basis of their own observations and abilities will opt for the methods of treatment which have proved most successful.

A patient can be treated in a number of ways: either by the gentle laying-on of the hands on a certain part of the body, or in the form of magnetic strokes (passes), which are also carried out with the hands over the patient. In this case it should be remembered that the hand is the best medium for the transference of the vital force, since the strongest emanations of Od come from it.

The Hand

There is an important physiological reason why the hands should be used to achieve the the the best healing results by the transference of vital energy: in the palm of the hand and the inner side of the fingers there are a large number of "Vater-Pacini" particles of lamellae, which were discovered in Wittenburg in 1741 by the anatomist, Abraham Vater (1684-1751), and rediscovered by Pacini in 1842. These are large terminal particles consisting of lamellae of the nerve fiber in the hypodermis for depth sensitivity.

Each of these formations encloses the end of a primitive nerve fiber with a delicate covering which can only be perceived under a microscope. By means of their structure and design, the Vater-Pacini particles work as a condensor to the nerves. The more of these there are in a part of the body, the more it can affect another system of nerves.

Mesmer too, recognized this fact, for he said: "The fluid radiates most powerfully from the inside of the hand." Reichenbach and all the later researchers confirmed this view. The best tool for healing magnetism is, therefore, the human hand of the practiced magnetopath who can heal with it.

Professor Schweninger, doctor to Bismarck for many years, wrote the following about healing magnetism and the hand of the therapist: "Whether it is a matter of warmth or emanation, it cannot be denied that certain people's hands possess power over certain other people." He said that this power is all the more effective if the person concerned has an innate medical character. With laying-on hands, or using them to stroke or hold, the hands can soothe pains and bring about changes in the surface parts of the tissue that have deep effects.

Undoubtedly Professor Schweninger's open-minded attitude to new methods of treatment had a lasting effect on the ideas of the founder of the German Empire, for even nowadays the following statement by Bismarck remains relevant: "Anyone who has been given the ability to heal by God or nature, cannot have this gift taken away from him by the police."

Polarity

According to the old proverb opposites attract. This is absolutely right because a force can only work when an opposing force is present. We can express this in a different way—there are positive and negative forces. In physics these two forces are referred to as plus (positive) and minus (negative), and the symbols (+) and (-) are familiar to us all from electricity. There is a positive and negative pole in the natural magnetic field produced by a magnetic iron, as well as in the artificial magnetic field produced by electricity. These two antipodes are called the North and South Pole after the poles of the earth. The earth itself is a huge magnet with a force field of around 0.5 gauss. All organic bodies constantly and spontaneously charge themselves in this field in order to develop the opposing polarity to the earth.

An electric current flows in the same way as the magnetic lines of force (from the negative to the positive pole) following a physical law; consequently a flow of force takes place. This movement of force can only take place between two unlike poles and never between two like poles. When we speak of positive and negative here, students should always keep in mind the concept of the physical law—positive and negative—in this book doesn't mean "good" and "bad."

The electrical principle applies to healing magnetism because every person is in himself positively and negatively polarized (otherwise no life processes could take place), only an outside influence upon the organism can occur only if the law of polarity is observed. The magnetizer must always treat the patient the wrong way round. Thus the right hand works upon the left side of the body and the left hand works upon the right side of the patient's body. When the middle of the body is treated, the hands of the practitioner form both poles, and the part of the body to be treated is taken between these two.

Following this cross-over rule, both hands have to be crossed when the back is treated or when the magnetizer stands behind the patient and treats him backwards, in order to keep the polarity preserved. This rule results in the fact that the transference of Od is more intensive in the case of people of the opposite sex than in people of the same sex.

THE PHYSICAL BODY

Anatomy is the basis of all endeavors in the medical or healing profession. The various parts and surfaces of the body should be learned in detail and memorized in order to make the descriptions of the individual holds and strokes, as well as their use in the practice of healing magnetism easier to understand, so that the correct places of application can easily be found. Thorough knowledge will save you time and tedious looking up of information later on. The word "anatomy" actually means "dissection."

Figure 12 and figure 13 (on page 52) show the regions of the human body. Classification makes it possible to determine the location of an injury or illness, for example, pains in the region of the heart or in the right upper part of the abdomen, etc. The body is divided into "planes." There are three planes which should be imagined as dividing the body vertically, and they are marked by lines shown in figure 14 on page 53.

The median plane, also called the sagittal or sagittal suture plane, divides the body into a left and a right half. The second plane is called the forehead or frontal plane because it runs parallel to the forehead and divides the body into a front and back part. It may also be called the transversal plane. (See figure 15 on page 54.)

Finally the body can be divided into any number of horizontal planes. In addition, a few other imaginary lines may be used to make location easier.

Since healing magnetism works on the nervous system in particular, it is important to know the paths of the most important nerves. (See figure 16 on page 55.) The nervous system is divided into the autonomic and the vegetative system, which interact with each other. Generally speaking, the autonomic system is subject to our will, whereas the vegetative system does not obey our will. We are interested only in peripheral parts of the system. The central nervous system consists of the brain and the spinal cord, the peripheral system of all those nerves which are found in the form of fibers of varying thicknesses. The following comparison should help you to imagine the fine ramifications of these nerves. If one were to dissolve the human body in an acid solution which would leave only the nerves intact, this would produce a structure with a consistency of cobwebs which would precisely define the person to whom this nervous system had once belonged.

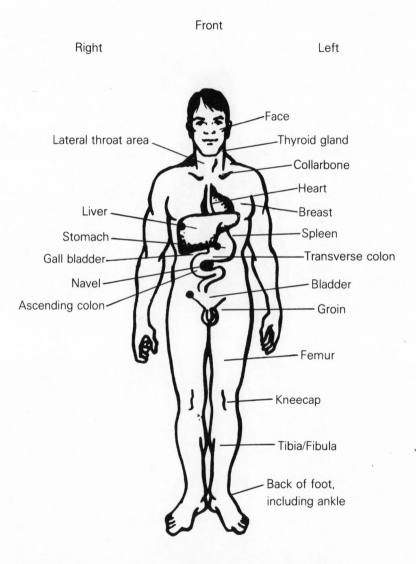

Figure 12. Organs and areas of the front of the body.

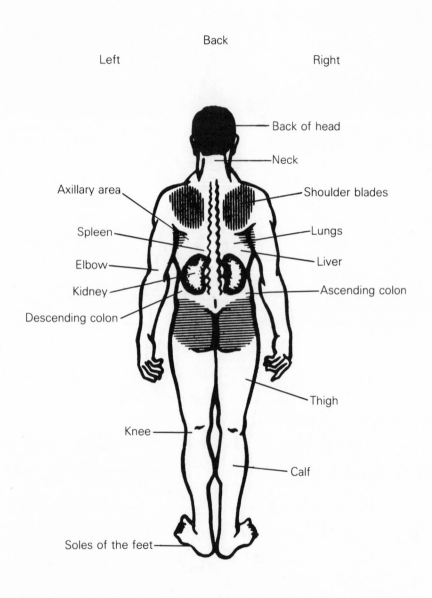

Figure 13. Organs and areas of the back of the body.

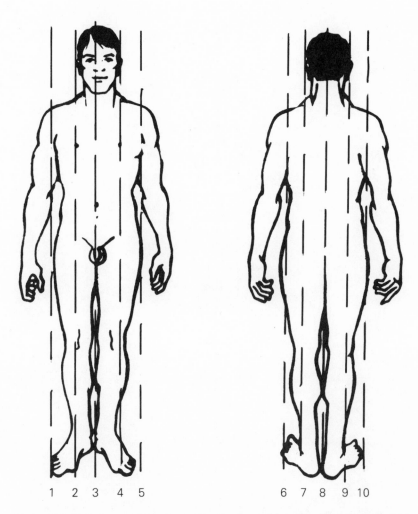

Figure 14. The planes of the body. On the front: 1) right axillary line; 2) right mammillary line; 3) median plane; 4) left mammillary line; 5) left axillary line. For the back of the body: 6) left axillary line; 7) left mammillary line; 8) median plane; 9) right mammillary line; 10) right axillary line.

Figure 15. The planes of the body. The forehead or frontal plane, also called the transverse plane. This may be subdivided into a left and right transversal line, which runs in a precise vertical line from the ear downward to the feet.

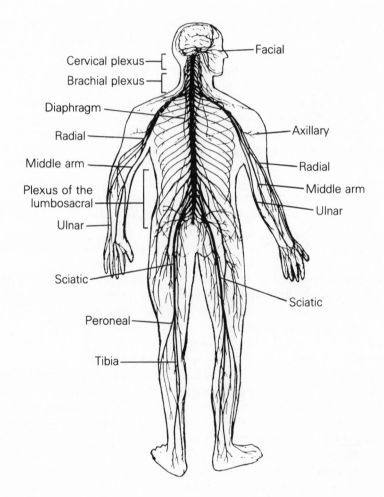

Figure 16. The nervous system.

THE NATURE OF ILLNESS

According to the theories of natural healing, illness is a form of disorder. In contrast to conventional medicine in which only the symptoms of an illness are treated, alternative medicine involves the whole person in the treatment. This kind of care is referred to as holistic medicine. A definite and integral part of holistic medicine is the recognition of causal correlations; this recognition aims at treating the causes of illness—the factors which trigger disease—as well as the symptoms and side effects.

An example may clarify this: if, as a result of constant irritation, someone suffers from stomach ulcers, it makes little sense to give the patient medicine to normalize the acid level in the stomach. It is also necessary to use appropriate methods to get rid of the irritation causing the illness. If this is not possible, the patient's psyche should be treated with appropriate and harmless biological medicines so that the irritation can no longer affect the stomach.

Organs functioning in a normal, healthy way presuppose a constant and sufficient presence of strengthening and life-preserving fluid energy. If there is too little vital magnetism, or its effect is diminished, the organs deteriorate in their function and a chemical disintegration ensues. If the influx of fluid energy in the body decreases or stops completely, then the organism ceases living; it dies and disintegrates into its organic components.

As a result of any illness, the entire organic system of the body falls into disarray. The flow of vital magnetism is disturbed. Illness, therefore, results from the lack (or inadequate circulation) of vital fluid in the body concerned. No medicine is capable of helping on its own; it only causes the sick organism to stimulate itself. In the science of natural healing we therefore think in terms of the activation of the body's own defense mechanisms which are released with the help of certain medicines or by other means. However, a cure can only ensue if there is sufficient fluid energy to produce the desired effect from the medication. In order to understand the connections, we could give the following comparison: of what use is a stove filled with combustible material without a match to light it?

On this topic Gerling wrote: "Neither the doctor nor the medicine effects a cure—it is the force which created us and maintains our life processes from the day we are born—and this force is the magnetism which has developed from universal magnetism to organic or animal magnetism."

How Does Healing Magnetism Work?

If an illness is treated with healing magnetism this does not mean that the patient will always recover, although he will very often find that the pain recedes immediately. Non-sensitive people may not feel anything during the transference of fluid. The following points often give rise to doubts about whether healing magnetism is having any effect, or whether it even exists. These doubts are most often felt by the patient, though they can also be felt by the healer.

Some patients have said they felt a very warm or cold flow during the magnetic healing treatment. Others maintain they felt tired during the treatment, or they were overcome by a feeling of weariness. They became aware of a great need for sleep, and this feeling persisted for several hours after treatment. Many patients report that they felt nothing at all.

It is better when an immediate effect is felt, but it is not essential. Frequently patients are relieved of great suffering without ever feeling the force that healed them. It is not necessary for every course of treatment with healing magnetism to produce a visible result straightaway. It is possible for the organ causing the pain to reveal the pain itself. This pain comes from the efforts made by the organ to relieve itself from the suffering.

In this context we can make a comparison with Huneke's neural therapy. Its starting point is that pain or illness is caused by so-called disruption fields (scars, injuries, damage to organs, etc.) which are apparently unconnected. By eliminating one of these disruption fields (using procain injections) spontaneous healing results—a phenomenon that takes place in seconds.

When this concept is applied to healing magnetism, it might be considered that the disruption fields are activated by it and consequently eliminated. An initial deterioration of condition also occurs in homeopathy and is always a good sign. It should not worry either the patient or the practitioner.

There are some chronic illnesses that have caused such strong organic disturbances that these can no longer be reversed, even with healing magnetism. However, in these desperate cases the transference of fluid energy can at least bring relief. The old adage, "prevention is better than cure," also applies with regard to the use of vital magnetism, because the earlier treatment is started, the better the prospect of permanent success. Used in a preventative way, a sensible course of therapy of healing magnetism can prevent serious illness from developing, or can at least considerably reduce its seriousness.

On this subject the healing magnetizer, Reinhold Gerling has said that it is unnatural to expect immediate help from magnetic healing. Although he knew of numerous cases where relief was achieved very quickly, he thinks we should submit to magnetic treatment with patience and perseverance. Most sick people only allow magnetic healing to take place when their systems are already exhausted. Time and patience are needed for the beneficial rays of the magnetism to become stronger so that they can effect the soul and the physical body.

THERAPY TRAINING

In this next section, you will be learning how to develop certain abilities that will help you become a magnetic healer. This involves learning how to "gaze" or visually tune into your patients. You will also need to learn some basic breathing exercises in order to transfer the magnetic healing force. Concentration exercises are important to therapy as well, for you need to develop self-confidence to stimulate and intensify the magnetic healing forces within so you can transfer it to other people. There exercises will benefit you on a personal level and allow you to transmit the highest amount of energy to your clients.

Learning the Odic Gaze

There is a great and wonderful power in a glance which can be transmitted to other people, particularly to the sensitive parts of the sick person's brain. The calmer, cleaner, and more confident the magnetizer's gaze, the stronger it will carry the will and become an enormous radiating source of Od. Reichenbach described this fact in his work, *The Sensitive Man*. In this work he proved that the emanation of the eyes is one of the strongest sources of Od which can be formed by the human organism.

We can frequently observe this effect in daily life: there are people who can captivate anybody with a glance and influence them in an irresistible way. Often these people are not aware of the powerful effect their eyes have, and if, during the course of the years, they have not noticed it, they cannot provide an adequate explanation of how it came about. Very few know that they possess the gift of the concentrated gaze, that concentrated magnetic gaze upon which their force is based.

Some people with Odic vision are confused with people who have "the evil eye." This is not to say that amongst people provided with the Od glance from birth, there are none with a bad character. There are even criminals who use this power. However, these are only a tiny minority compared with what we call healing sensitive people.

There are not many who are actually born with the gift of the Odic magnetic gaze. Nature has made provisions here, for these forces are present in all of us. It is merely a question of arousing them and stimulating them with appropriate exercises so that we can apply them sensibly and for the benefit of our fellow men.

Various textbooks on healing magnetism repeatedly refer to personal magnetism. Expressions like "magnetic gaze," "Odic gaze," or "central or concentrated gaze," refer to the same type of look. All these terms mean the same thing: the Odic gaze is the link between the central gaze and the concentration of thought.

Start by looking the patient in the eyes. You will often find that your eyes cannot be "met." Under no circumstances force a patient to look at you. When you notice that your look is being avoided, look at the base of the patient's nose or chest. It is not necessary for the patient to keep his eyes open. It can even happen that he drops off to sleep; this will frequently happen with very weak patients. If this is the case, complete the treatment and leave the patient asleep. In general he will wake up after a short while feeling stronger. More-over, the fixation should be maintained for the entire duration of the treatment. By practicing the exercises, you will be able to sense what is wrong with a patient—even when he cannot tell you. This will help a great deal in the healing process.

Gazing Exercises

The following exercises will help you to prepare and train your eyes:

1. Take out the page with the black dot in the middle, (see page 185 at the end of the book) and stick it to a wall at eye level. Sit down on a chair about nine feet from the wall. Relax and stare at the dot for a minute without blinking. After a minute, stop for a while. When you have rested your eyes, repeat the exercise another five times.

2. Then fix the sheet of paper about three feet to the right and return to the same sitting position as before. Keep your head turned to the place where the sheet was attached before; now fix your eyes on the present position of the black dot, without moving your head. Repeat this exercise five times for a minute each time.

It is better to increase the length of the exercise slowly and steadily, rather than train to the point of exhaustion. Nevertheless, try to practice this form of training at least once a day, even if only for a few minutes. After a short time you will find that your eye muscles and your eye nerves are becoming noticeably stronger and more per-severing. When your eyes have become accustomed to the ex-ercises, it is time to practice the "central gaze:"

3. Sit down in front of a mirror and stare at your face without moving your head, and if possible, without blinking. With both eyes, stare at the base of your nose in your reflection. If you find this difficult, you could start by drawing a small dot at the base of your nose with an eyebrow pencil. Gaze at this dot every day for about three minutes. After three or four days, increase the length of time you stare at the dot by one minute; the following day increase it by another minute and so on, until you have reached fifteen minutes.

At the beginning of the exercise you will probably see only the dot clearly and distinctly, while the rest of the face is blurred. However, if you carry out the exercise with concentration and perseverance, you will manage to see your face and the area immediately around it clearly, and not blurred. When you have reached this point, practice the central gaze without the help of a specially marked dot, but simply by staring at the base of your nose in the mirror. As soon as you master the gaze, you no longer need the reflection, but you can now apply it in a practical way for magnetic healing treatment.

4. After a short break, attach the sheet of paper with the dot three feet to the left on the wall. Sit down again as you were at the beginning, and stare at the dot for one minute without moving your head and without blinking. After a short break, repeat this exercise another four times.

5. Another exercise for fixing the gaze consists of attaching the sheet of paper to a wall at eye level when you are in a standing position. Stand in front of it and keep your eyes fixed firmly on the dot. Now turn your head slowly as far as you can to the right and then to the left, without letting your gaze slip. Again, repeat this exercise five times with short breaks in between.

Carry on by taking your starting position again. When your gaze has settled, make circular clockwise movements with your head, while constantly keeping your eyes on the dot. After five tries, each lasting a minute (always with short breaks in between), repeat the whole procedure using counter-clockwise movements.

6. As a final exercise, stand with your back to the opposite wall and again stare at the dot. Without moving the head, let your gaze wander from the upper left corner of the room to the upper right corner, and then slowly to the bottom right, from there to the bottom left, and from there back to the top left. Repeat the exercise five times, taking a minute each time and with corresponding breaks in between.

In case you find the exercises too strenuous at first, shorten the length of time of each one and do not try to force yourself to finish all the exercises through to the end.

However, only use this gaze technique when you talk to patients or carry out treatments. Avoid using it when patients are talking to you, as they might become insecure and unable to express themselves clearly. Increase the effect of the central gaze by talking clearly and intelligibly. Moreover, the central gaze can give you a greater sense of security and self-confidence in daily life, and it can help you to fulfill many an honest wish.

Breathing Exercises

Human beings can survive for a while without food, but not without oxygen. Oxygen, which is essential for life, is in the air we breathe. If the supply of oxygen to the brain is interrupted for any reason, the sensitive brain cells die within five minutes. The parts of the brain which have died as a result of lack of oxygen cannot be regenerated and the damage caused is irreversible. The entire organism is therefore dependent on a constant supply of oxygen. And yet most people breathe incorrectly and insufficiently because they do not take enough time to breathe properly and don't even know how to do it.

A new-born baby takes about fifty to sixty breaths per minute; a five year old child takes about thirty, and an adult is satisfied with only sixteen to twenty breaths per minute, although the need for oxygen is about three times that amount. The "hunger for oxygen" of civilized man results from the air pollution of our technical age. As breathing is closely related to the output of the magnetic healing force during the magnetizing process, it is important to pay attention to good breathing during treatment.

Anyone who has practiced relaxation through self–hypnosis or yoga knows that breathing is of great importance for health. Yoga, in particular, has made the teaching of correct breathing into a science, known as Hatha Yoga.

This book is not intended to deal with this old Indian science in great detail. There is already a vast amount of literature on yoga and the techniques of correct breathing. Anyone who wishes to improve or perfect his personal magnetism can refer to the relevant literature. For the prospective healing magnetizer it is sufficient to be skilled in breathing in and out, and to regulate the breathing to the magnetic strokes and treatments.

Most people nowadays breathe incorrectly, i.e., their breathing is too shallow. Moreover, a large number of people nowadays spend too little time in the fresh air and most of their time in rooms or towns where the air conditions are far from ideal. In addition, there is frequently a lack of oxygen and too little humidity.

You can do breathing exercises in a quiet room at home with the window open, as long as the outside air is not polluted (for instance, not near an industrial site or a power station). It is better to exercise in the open air where you will be undisturbed (for example, if you are lucky enough to own a garden). For the breathing exercises it is best to bare the chest. Should this be impossible because it's too cold, then wear clothing that is as light as possible for the conditions.

You should have a clock that shows seconds. Sit down comfortably and put the watch in front of you. Let your arms hang loosely and dangle your hands a few times as if you were shaking something off. Take care to ensure that the position of your body is completely relaxed, push your chest forward and keep your head straight. Now breathe through the nose evenly and quietly. Breathe in to the count of three seconds. Now hold your breath for three seconds and then breathe out for three seconds. This is a breathing cycle lasting a total of nine seconds.

Practice this exercise for ten minutes a day for a week. For each ten minutes of exercising time there are about sixty-five breathing cycles, each lasting nine seconds. At the end of a week increase the time for breathing in, for holding the breath, and for breathing out to five seconds each, so that one breathing cycle now lasts fifteen seconds.

At first you might experience a slight feeling of giddiness, tiredness or of feeling unwell during the exercises. However, there is no cause for alarm; it merely shows that up to now you have been breathing incorrectly. If this happens, stop the exercise and repeat it after a break.

When practicing breathing exercises, the beginner should not overdo it. It is better to increase one's performance slowly until a certain standard is reached.

Concentration Exercises

Good practitioners have to have confidence in themselves and in the method of treatment. They have to be convinced that they are capable of healing. As soon as each of you have achieved your first healing successes you will gain self–confidence. This will increase your effectiveness and the results will improve even more. Success reinforces the magnetic force and leads to even better results. Doubts about your own powers and ability will always have a detrimental effect.

Control of the thought processes is a fundamental prerequisite to stimulate and intensify the magnetic healing forces and the ability to transfer them to other people. What are thoughts? Thoughts are forces which enter our consciousness and activate a mysterious process and can have a positive or a negative effect. Thus, our thoughts can be useful or harmful, they can help or hinder us.

Thoughts are often described as being good, bad, wicked, false, loving, etc. This means that thoughts can be animated with any some extent, given them the form of a fine substance with is a real as light, warmth or electricity. This means that thoughts are fluid formations of elemental material. The more powerfully and intensely a thought enters our consciousness, the more we animate and activate it. When the thought has been registered in the memory, we radiate and transmit it. However, the thought is always linked to its creator by a kind of mental bond. When it is transmitted, a thought is inclined to join up with other similar thoughts. The sum of similar thoughts adds up to a powerful group of thoughts that becomes more animated, the more it is attracted to likeminded people.

Thoughts are often described as being good, bad, wicked, false, loving etc. This means that thoughts can be animated with any feeling or emotion. When the thoughts are animated with anxiety, sorrow, worry, dejection, or hatred, i.e., with negative concepts, they will join up with thoughts of the same type that have been emanated and they will consequently have a much stronger effect. Thoughts of fear and anxiety in turn attract thoughts of a similar kind, so that you are not only troubled by your own thoughts, but also by those of other people.

When you intend to do something, you should replace the feeling of doubt, "I can't do it," with a confident, firm, and fearless

"I can." In this way you will succeed in your endeavors. Similarly jealous and envious thoughts will come back to you with other identical thoughts, and they will trouble you as long as you have not managed to overcome them. Angry thoughts will always arouse anger in other people if you do not reject such thoughts.

The same applies in reverse: goodwill, love, courage, strength, confidence, success, tolerance, joy, i.e., any positive qualities, join up with equally effective groups of thoughts which come back to us. Therefore we constantly have to try to think only in a positive way and to keep our negative thoughts under control, or better still, not let them arise in the first place. Control over thought is the key to the gate of the psychic forces. In order to control thought, one must first learn how to concentrate on a particular thought. This form of concentration aims at the absolute mastery of a thought or of a thread of thoughts to the exclusion of all external impressions, so that you are totally absorbed in the task at hand.

In order to exercise intellectual concentration, you need a quiet room where you will not be disturbed. Loud traffic noises or the sounds of other occupants in the house are distracting for the beginner, and you will find it difficult to "get into" the basic exercises. It goes without saying that the telephone and doorbell should be disconnected during the exercises and you should have no spectators.

Draw up a timetable in which you include a daily practice period, if possible, always at the same time. The best time for exercise is in the morning, when body and mind are rested and should not tire too quickly. You should only exercise during the afternoon or evening in an absolute emergency, as the body usually requires some rest at that time and it is very easy to nod off after exercising for a short while. For this reason there should be a bed or a couch where you can lie down.

It should be emphasized that this exercise room is only required at the beginning. Anyone who has mastered the concentration of thought is totally unaffected by disturbing noises from the outside world and by external impressions, and is able to concentrate amidst the greatest turmoil.

In order to be able to concentrate effectively, you first have to learn to come to grips with physical restlessness. As a first step it is important to completely relax all your muscles. For this it is necessary to stop all nervous movements which may actually be an unconscious activity. For example, you might have the habit of constantly playing with your hands, or scratching your face, or putting your finger in your ear. In this case it is necessary to begin by eliminating these nervous habits. To do this, take an interesting book, put it on a table in from of you, open it and sit straight in front of it, relaxed. Now put the palm of your hand on the edge of the table, the thumb pointing downwards. (This is how children used to have to sit when they started school.) Remain in this position while you read for as long as possible. (When turning the page you can of course move one hand briefly.) Repeat the exercise whenever you read. At first you will find it rather difficult to keep your hand still. However, the more you practice this exercise, the longer you will be able to remain in this position.

You can develop exercises which are tailored to your own bad habits. There are no limits on your imagination. It is important that all the exercises are the opposite of the habit which you are attempting to eliminate.

There are some exercises which you can carry out in public. Let us suppose that you are in the habit of turning your head straightaway in the direction where you think a noise came from. This can be a very irritating habit for a beginner. In this case, take a book, or better still, some writing that you have to learn, and sit down on a bench in a park, in a railway station, or in any busy place, i.e., somewhere crowded and noisy. While you are reading or learning, do not let yourself be disturbed in any way by noise, whether it is caused by passing pedestrians, playing children, hooting or braking cars, barking dogs or anything else.

At first you will be able to tolerate this situation for five or ten minutes at most without letting yourself be distracted. In the course of time you will react as calmly and with as much discipline as is necessary. Thus the first prerequisite to concentration is the exclusion of all noise, sounds, images, and thoughts coming from the outside. The principle of concentration consists of being able to hold onto a specific thought to the exclusion of all others.

When beginners have relaxed physically, they can start with the proper exercises of concentration for the control of thought. For the individual exercises, set apart a certain period of time—for instance, start with five minutes a day, increase to ten and work up to a maximum of fifteen minutes. When you have managed to concentrate for fifteen minutes while eliminating all distracting thoughts, you have achieved your goal. (There are people, especially those who do a lot of yoga, who can carry out these exercises for hours. For our purposes this is completely unnecessary.) When you are able to control your thoughts, it is enough to do a short concentration exercise once or twice a day for about one or two minutes in order to remain mentally alert all the time.

You can use an alarm clock or a timer which can be set for the required period of time. The end of the concentration period should be indicated with a signal. If the alarm is very loud, it is advisable not to place the clock directly next to the exercising place as the ringing will startle you. However, this does not matter once you have progressed sufficiently with the concentration of your thoughts. At that point you will no longer need an alarm clock in your exercise room.

During the first week, practice for five minutes a day, during the second week increase this to ten minutes, and in the third week to fifteen minutes every day. Set your alarm clock for this period of time.

You now need a specific theme for the exercises. Perhaps you have made a long journey or have undertaken a weekend trip. You might have seen an interesting film which fascinated you. When you have decided upon a specific topic or theme, sit down comfortably in a chair. You can also lie down on the sofa and exercise while lying down. What is important is that you are completely relaxed and that your muscles are entirely loosened up. Breathe deeply in and out regularly as described before. The concentration of thought should accompany the even and deep breathing.

Now imagine the course of your chosen theme in full detail. Try to recreate the event in your mind in all its most minute details. Single out a strong point of reference with which to begin: for instance, how you got into the car to set off on your journey.

At first you will very quickly finish thinking about your theme and will realize that you have omitted many details which you could not recall at that moment. If you go on repeating the exercise using this same theme, you will notice that you have many more details stored in your memory which you can now recall.

When you have concentrated on past events and are in a position to recapitulate these precisely and reconstruct them in detail in your mind, you can start to concentrate on your future activity as a healing magnetizer. However, before doing this you have to master the technique of the healing magnetic strokes and holds, and know when you can apply them.

It is up to the individual to choose the order in which he works through the various chapters and exercises. However, you should only carry out healing magnetism treatment when you feel sure of all the disciplines.

As soon as you master the concentration of thought, you should aim to transfer as much of your fluid energy as possible to patients during the therapy. On the other hand, you will have to try to remove as much as possible of the superfluous and sick Od from patients, and have a calming effect on them using the negative treatment.

Most healing magnetizers report that during the course of treatment they experience a sucking sensation at their fingertips, as if something were flowing out. Others define this sensation as driving through a dense net of cobwebs; still others describe it as the feeling that they are wading into or driving through a syrupy mass. No matter how the emanation of vital energy is experienced, once you have personally developed sufficient healing magnetic forces, you will yourself notice and feel when you are transferring the fluid energy.

LEARNING THE TREATMENTS

When you look ahead to Part 3, you will see that I have described a number of common ailments that many people have, and in the description I have included a method of treatment. The section that follows here shows you how to do the treatments in Part 3. We will discuss positive and negative treatments, special treatments, how to stroke the body, how to draw off energy from the body magnetically, and how to make both positive and negative magnetic water.

Positive Treatment

Positive treatment has a more or less strong stimulating effect (to some extent even an exciting effect) on the patient. The term "toning up" was introduced in nature healing to describe this effect. The positive strokes are reinforced by the mental concentration of the will on the fingertips and the thumbs to stimulate and intensify the emanation of the magnetic force, and by the fixation of the patient during the treatment.

Using your concentration, you set the Od forces, the vital fluid, into motion. During the course of the magnetic healing treatment, this passes from your body, through your fingertips and into the body to which it is transmitted; in the case of general magnetic healing treatment, it is consequently transmitted directly to the patient; when activating drinks or any other objects, it is transferred to these.

Therefore during the treatment your mental concentration must have the sole aim of bringing the sick person relief, help, and healing by passing on and transferring the vital force. Your healing magnetic forces will be particularly activated by mental concentration.*

With the positive treatment the therapist's hand may touch the patient's skin, but only very lightly. Pressure should not be exerted under any circumstances. Never let the positive stroking degenerate into a kind of "massage," since that would jeopardize the whole success of the treatment. Nor is it necessary to lay on the surface of the hand. The fingertips, and if necessary, the tips of the thumbs are sufficient. The lighter the touch, the more gliding the movement, the better the results will be.

When the patient is sitting down, you stand in front of him, face to face. The distance should be calculated so that you can easily touch him with outstretched hands. If you treat him while he is lying down, stand to the left of where he is lying with your legs slightly apart. (As we have already noted: to achieve perfect treatment the

---

*Note: Mental concentration is not a prerequisite, because with the appropriate movements, the emanation of the fluid takes place in accordance with a law of nature, i.e., with correct polarity the forces will always flow to the opposite pole until there is a balance. There is, however, a difference, because the restoration of the fluid balance can take place slowly and sluggishly or quickly and vigorously. Besides, each healing magnetic session would then last for several hours.

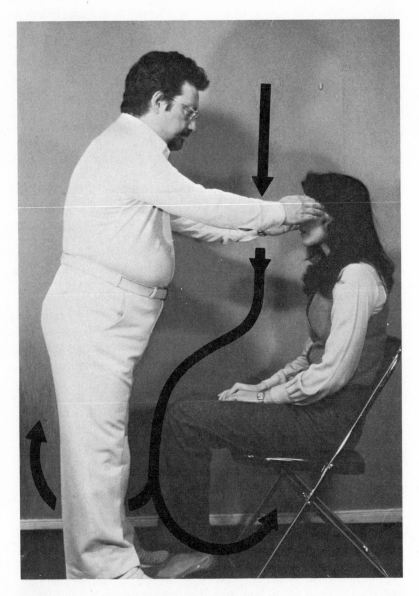

Figure 17. The start of a positive treatment in a sitting position. My back is facing south and the patient's back is facing north.

back of the patient's head should face north and his face should point south.)

Now put your hands in correct polarity on the patient's forehead. The right hand should be on the left side of the forehead, and vice-versa. (See figure 17.) The tips of your index and middle fingers should touch each other lightly in the middle of the forehead. Now move your hands slowly towards the feet. Move them gently over the cheeks (see figure 18), then over the lateral region of the neck outwards, along the axial line further down, on the outside of the thigh, down to the feet. Then slowly remove both hands to the left and right, bring them round in a wide curve back to the patient's forehead and begin again with the lengthwise strokes. On no account should you bring the hands back to the starting point in a straight line or the effect will be nullified.

When you have done about seven to nine strokes, have a short break of one or two minutes. Then repeat the manipulation. On average, twenty-one to forty-nine strokes are sufficient.

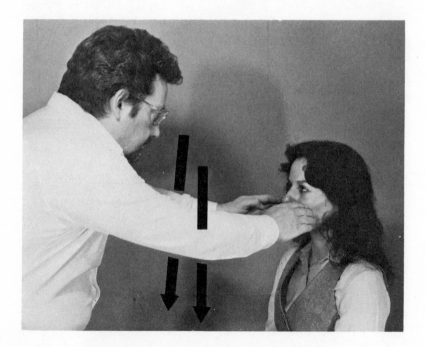

Figure 18. Positive treatment. See the light touch of the hands.

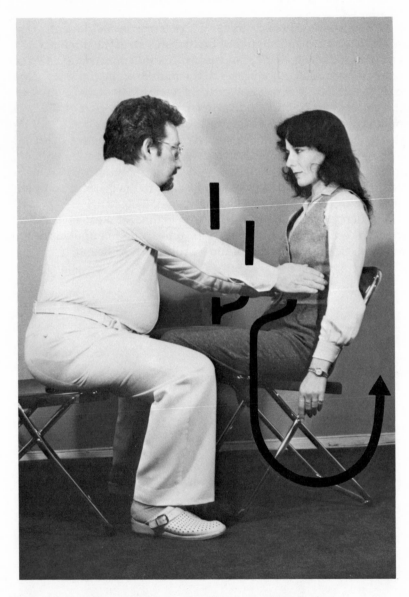

Figure 19. Positive treatment on the upper part of the body.

We have already noted that over a period of years every magne-tizer develops his own style. It is therefore not necessary to follow the indicated directions of the strokes religiously, and in positive treatment you are free to follow the course of the nerves. (See figure 16 on page 55.) The decisive factor is always how you can achieve the best healing results and which kind of treatment you perform best.

A magnetic healing treatment session should last for at most twenty minutes. Treatment is often given under the mistaken im-pression that the more of it there is, the better. However, this does not apply to healing magnetism. When the therapist feels mentally and physically tired, he can cause more harm than good. It's better to split the treatment up into several shorter sessions than to try to cram in as much as possible into one session.

During the treatment, keep your eyes firmly on the patient whether he has his eyes open or shut. Concentrate your gaze on the base of his nose, as described in the chapter on "fixation."

Since the fluid force penetrates through clothes, the patient does not necessarily have to be undressed. He should simply not be wearing too many clothes, otherwise he would not be able to feel the light effect of the touching. Thick coats and similar items of clothing do not completely cancel out the effect of the magnetic force, but they certainly have a weakening effect and should therefore be removed before treatment. Make sure that during the magnetic manipulation the muscles of your arms and hands are completely relaxed.

When you have precisely followed the requirements and rules for the positive treatment, you will feel a kind of sucking feeling at your fingertips when the strokes are administered; some prac-titioners also feel a slight tingling, as if something were flowing out of their fingers.

Each lengthwise stroke over an adult should last on average about thirty seconds (approximately 10%). You have to coordinate the speed at which you let your hands slide from the patient's head to his feet to correspond with the time given above. This will always present difficulties to the beginner, since people vary in body height. With children and small people the rate of the execution of the strokes has to be slowed down, and with tall people it has to be speeded up. In fact, speeding up or slowing down only makes a difference of a fraction of a second. Before you carry out your first healing magnetic treatment session, you should practice the strokes and the time sequence. The section on "therapy training" explains how to do this.

However, it should be emphasized that the recommended time of thirty seconds per stroke lengthwise is only a rough guide which can be increased or decreased within certain limits. The only decisive factor is the effect on the patient. There is a danger that if the strokes are too fast or too light, the positive treatment may turn into negative treatment. This will have exactly the opposite of the desired effect.

Positive treatment is recommended particularly for those illnesses which are connected with a weakening or a blockage of the body's own fluid circulation. Disorders in the functioning of the individual organs, malfunctioning problems with the secretion of metabolic waste, nervous states of irritability, a damaged immunity system (the body's defense mechanism against infectious diseases) or any illness requiring more fluid energy may be favorably influenced by positive magnetization. (See figure 19 on page 72.) Thus positive healing magnetic treatment has a restorative and toning effect.

For the sake of completeness, we should point out that many renowned healing magnetizers and magnetopaths "breathe upon" the patient before and after the positive treatment, in accordance with the old school of thought. However, we consider that on our time we should forego that practice for reasons of hygiene, especially as the same results can be achieved with the methods described here.

Negative Treatment

In contrast to the positive method of treatment, negative treatment consists of short, quick strokes from the head down to the patient's feet. This form of treatment should take place in a relaxed way without any tension of the muscles and the will. Whereas positive treatment replaces the fluid energy lacking in the patient, negative therapy removes the excess. Unlike the positive treatment, the patient's body is not touched during negative manipulation. The magnetizer's hands carry out the strokes over the body at a distance of three to ten inches.

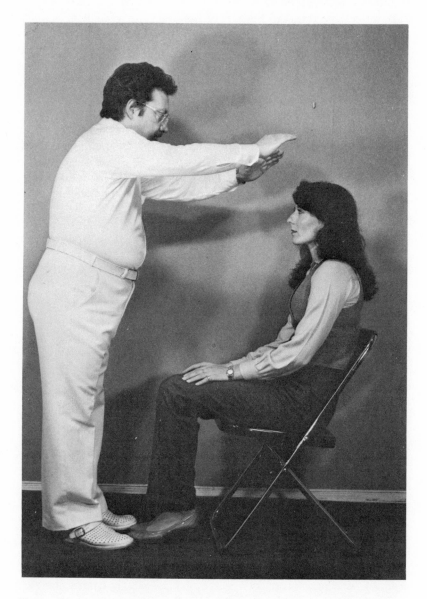

Figure 20. Starting position for the negative treatment in a sitting position.

When the patient is sitting down, stand about three feet in front of him in a relaxed position. (See figure 20 on page 75.) If the patient is lying down, stand to the left of his bed with your legs casually supported. Your arms should be held loosely, roughly over the patient's stomach. Now breathe in deeply and at the same time lift your arms slightly (as shown in figure 21 and let your hands hang completely loose and relaxed. Now bring your arms over the patient's head and pass them slowly to his feet. At the same time breathe out calmly. (See figure 22.)

The rate of the strokes is related to the time you need to breathe out. Breathing out should certainly not be shortened or lengthened. Breathing comes completely naturally and calmly, as described in the section on "Therapy Training." Before each magnetic stroke, take a breath and carry out the stroke while slowly breathing out. (See figures 23 and 24 on pages 78 and 79.)

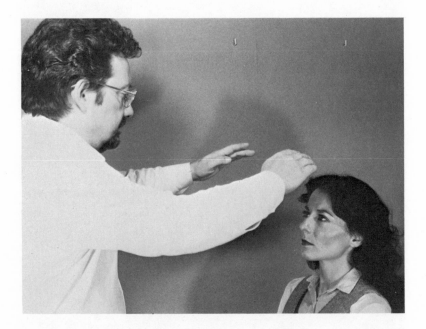

Figure 21. Negative treatment. The therapist should breathe in deeply while lifting the arms slightly, as shown here.

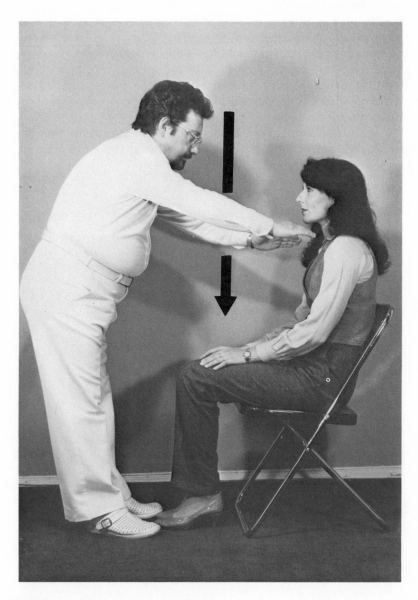

Figure 22. Negative magnetic stroke.

After each stroke carried out over the patient's feet, you have to shake out your hands. For that you turn away from the patient, clench your hands into a fist and bend your elbows. Now with both hands make a shaking movement, and at the end of the movement, open your clenched hands as though you were throwing something away (see figure 25 on page 80). This shaking causes the bad fluid energy, the harmful sick substances which the magnetizer has carried away through the negative treatment, to be removed from the patient and from himself.

Negative treatment should last no longer than twenty minutes per session. At the beginning you will notice that the movements,

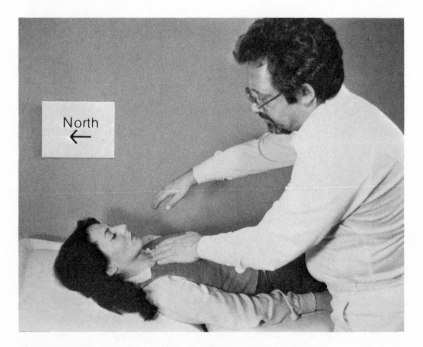

North
←

Figure 23. Note the direction of the stroke here.

and above all, the handing over of your own vital force, will weaken you considerably. Always remember: a sick or weak healing magnetizer should not treat any patients until he has fully recovered himself, or when he is not in complete possession of his physical and fluid strength. A practitioner who has overexerted himself during the treatment has to wait until his reserves of strength have been built up again through natural sleep.

No harm is done if you finish the treatment after five or ten minutes. On the contrary, it is better to magnetize for a short while with full transference of force than for a longer time with little strength.

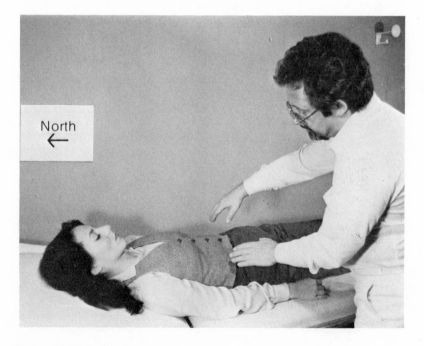

Figure 24. The direction of the stroke.

The negative treatment is beneficial for illnesses requiring "draining off" therapy. These include inflammations, fevers, states of agitation and anxiety, convulsions, irritations.

Neutralization

Whether you were using the positive or the negative magnetic healing therapy, at the end of every session carry out a few neutral strokes (also known as "cross strokes"). These final strokes serve to shake off the superfluous fluid which is clinging to the patient. You should also indicate that the treatment is over.

This "neutralization" is carried out in the following way: bring both your hands closer to the patient's face, curved slightly, so that the fingertips touch lightly. Now quickly pull the hands and

Figure 25. Shaking your hands causes any harmful sick substances to be removed from both the patient and the therapist.

arms away from each other. You are making a sort of flinging movement to the left and to the right, so that at the end of the movement both arms are spread out. When you have done this, stretch your fingers as if you wanted to throw away something you have pulled apart (see figure 26). The cross strokes should be carried out in front of the patient's face at a distance of three to eight inches. As a rule three to five neutral strokes are sufficient to finish off a treatment.

After each magnetic healing session the therapist should wash his hands thoroughly under running water to eliminate any bad fluid that might possibly remain. Running water has the best drawing off effect, quite apart from the fact that it is necessary to wash your hands after each treatment for reasons of hygiene.

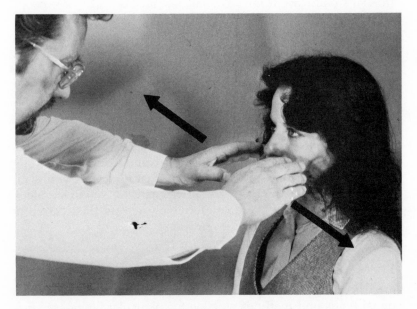

Figure 26. Neutralization should be done at the end of any session, whether you are working with positive or negative treatment.

If you have carried out the treatment in the open air, perhaps as a first aid measure, and there is no running water nearby, you can either put your hands on a tree as if you were embracing the trunk, or place both your hands on the ground. Both these possibilities have a good drawing off effect as a provisional measure.

Stroking Exercises

Before starting on the magnetizing process, you should take a few breaths, applying the fifteen second cycle. In time you will develop a sense of how long a fifteen second cycle lasts, so that you will not need to clock yourself any more. This sense of time will become so deep rooted as a result of constant exercise that you will be able to rely on it.

When using positive magnetism, stroking an adult from head to foot should last about thirty seconds; when using the negative stroke it should last as long as it takes to breathe out. Since people vary in height, you have to determine the speed of the positive stroke so that you need about thirty seconds to stroke the length of the body (approximately 10%).

Stand to the left of the place of treatment, while watching the clock, and practice the corresponding lengthways strokes. After some intensive exercise you will develop a sense of the correct timing for different heights and for the speed with which the strokes should be carried out.

It should be emphasized once more that the rules about time should not be rigidly adhered to as this could result in tension in some cases. As a magnetizer, this is the last thing that you want. Always proceed on the basis that all magnetic treatment should be carried out in a relaxed and comfortable way. For this reason, do some limbering-up exercises to stay agile.

Special Treatment

Apart from the general positive and negative treatments, there are special holds and methods suitable for particular illnesses. These could be referred to a partial, local treatment. The special treatment can have an additional intensive effect upon the individual organs, glands or joints to supplement the general treatment. Strong pains, states of excitement, anxiety or weakness are controlled more rapidly this way.

When using the special holds you have to pay particular attention to the polarity. Thus the magnetizer's right hand always treats the patient's left side up to the saggital line, i.e., up to the middle of the body. The left hand should magnetize the right half of the body in exactly the same way.

Older works on magnetic healing repeatedly include descriptions of the special holds without paying any attention to the polarity. With these holds the magnetizer usually stands behind the patient (who is either sitting or standing). The magnetizer carries out the holds, following the same poles, i.e., he treats the patient's right side with his right hand, and the patient's left side with his left hand. These manipulations may have a certain calming and perhaps cooling effect, but hardly any exchange of fluid force takes place. Therefore a detailed description of the holds has been deliberately omitted so as not to confuse the learner.

If you treat the patient from the back, so that you are standing behind him, you must always make sure that the polarity is preserved according to the cross-over law. In this instance you can only treat with your hands crossed.

With most of the holds, stand to the left of the patient to treat parts on the front side of his body. In this case it is always the magnetizer's right hand which performs the manipulations and the holds. The left hand lies on the patient's back as an opposite pole, i.e., always on that half of the body which is opposite to the one that is being treated. So when you are treating the left front half of the body (always with your right hand), your left hand should lie at the same height on the right back half of the body, and vice-versa. You must always make sure that the polarity is preserved. When you are treating the right front half of the body, use the left hand—the right hand then forms the opposite pole. In this instance you obviously stand to the right of the patient. You achieve the best results if, as far as possible, you avoid crossing over the sagittal line of both halves of the body with the hand that is treating while you are manipulating.

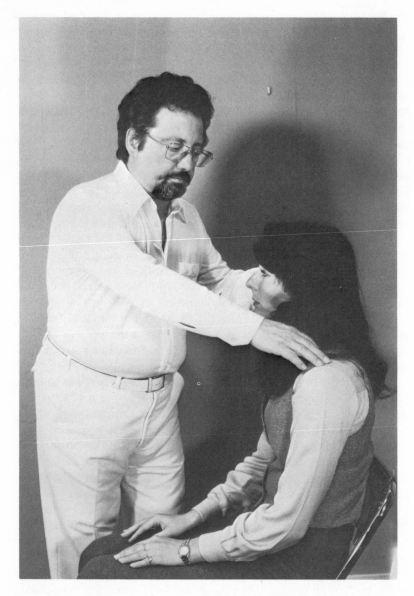

Figure 27. Localized partial stroke treatment of left shoulder joint.

Partial and Local Treatment

These partial strokes are used in the case of illnesses of specific parts of the body, for example, illness in the joints. (See figure 27.) The strokes themselves are carried out by starting above the part of the body concerned, and slowly working towards the bottom. The strokes should always start from the parts requiring treatment and gradually diminish. Positive or negative strokes can be used, depending on the nature of the illness. After each partial stroke, the hand being used for the treatment is pulled back to the starting point in a wide curve.

The duration of treatment per session is about three to five minutes. In the case of partial strokes, it is also better not to make the individual treatment too long, but to treat the patient frequently. Moreover, you should take into account the fact that in principle a general treatment, whether positive or negative, precedes or follows on from each partial treatment.

The length of time taken for treatment can vary. If, for example, you know that you will follow general treatment with a special magnetization, or if a special treatment precedes the general therapy, the magnetizing time will altogether last twenty minutes. A total treatment time of twelve to fifteen minutes has, in practice, proved to be best.

Stroking the Back

It has already been pointed out that in order to magnetize successfully it is important to take into account the polarizing ratios according to the cross-over law. For example, when you stand behind a patient to treat his back, you find yourself in the same state of polarity as him, for in this case the right part of his body corresponds with the right side of your body. In order to achieve an opposite polarization, you have to cross your hands while giving the treatment. (See figure 28 on page 86.)

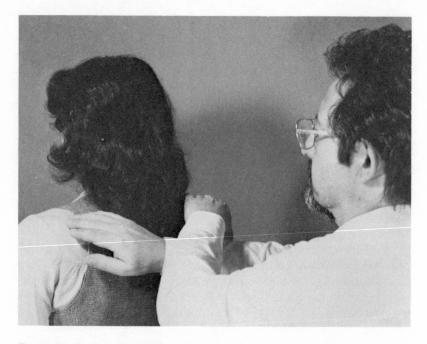

Figure 28. Cross your hands while treating the back or you will lose polarity. You do not have to cross your hands when you face your patient and treat from the front.

It is beneficial to follow the anatomical course of the nervous system while carrying out the strokes. The strokes take place as indicated, slowly from the top to the bottom.

The back hold is suitable for the treatment of any illnesses in the region of the vertebral column and the shoulder. The back stroke with crossed arms can easily be carried out on patients who are lying down. In this case the sick person is lying in bed or on the couch on his stomach. The magnetizer stands or sits to the patient's left at about the height of the thigh. This makes it easier to include the entire vertebral column and the region of the hip and the hollow of the knee in the treatment.

For treating the sciatic nerve, start the stroke somewhere above the hip region, then bring it slowly over the middle of the buttocks further down, along the back of the thigh, through the hollows of the knees, over the calves to the middle of the heel. Slowly withdraw your crossed arms from the patient's body, turn sideways and uncross your arms. Then slightly raise your trunk, cross your arms again and start with the next stroke at the starting point of the treatment.

If the sciatic nerve is acutely inflamed, it is best to carry out the treatment as a negative treatment. The direction of the strokes stays the same as in the positive treatment; the only difference is that during treatment the patient's body is not touched and the speed of the strokes should be faster. Moreover, in between the individual strokes you should shake out your hands. The best time to do this is when you are turned away from the patient and are uncrossing your arms. The duration of treatment for all the strokes described should be approximately three to five minutes.

Stroking the Eye

The patient is seated in a chair in a comfortable and relaxed position. The practitioner stands on the right side and puts the fingertips of his right hand lightly on the patient's left eye socket. The fingertips of the left hand lie on the right eye socket. The hands should be laid on very gently (see figure 29 on page 88). The patient should feel no pressure whatsoever. The stroke must be carried out extremely lightly.

It is necessary for the patient to sit up high so that the magnetizer can perform the treatment in as relaxed and unrestrained a manner as possible. For this stroke the height of the seat should be adapted to the height of the patient and to the practitioner, if possible, either by using a low stool or by putting a cushion on the chair. The eye treatment brings relief to all diseases of the eye, as well as to the treatment of migraine conditions. The duration of the treatment should be approximately three minutes.

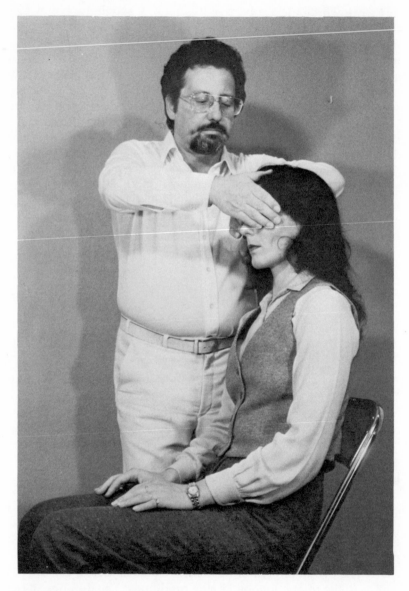

Figure 29. Gentle eye treatment.

Stroking the Forehead

The therapist is again standing sideways to the right of the patient, who is seated comfortably on a chair. The magnetizer puts his left hand lightly on the patient's neck; the right hand rests on his forehead without exerting any pressure, so that he feels the contact only very slightly. (See figure 30 on page 90.)

In some of the older works on healing magnetism the forehead, the eye and the ear movements—as well as those for the back and chest—are always described with the magnetizer standing behind the patient and reaching over him to treat him on the front. It must be emphasized once again that the transference through movements like this cannot do any harm therapeutically, but at best it can only give the patient a feeling of reassurance. Because of the incorrect polarization with this kind of movement there can be virtually no magnetic healing effect or transference of the fluid force. (Always remember that with healing magnetic treatment the greatest attention should be paid to the polarity, since this is very important for achieving successful results.) Stroking the forehead correctly is especially important for the treatment of headaches in the region of the forehead, the base of the nose and the frontal sinus.

The duration of treatment is about three to five minutes, depending on the severity of the case.

Stroking the Ear

The patient is again seated and relaxed on a chair. The practitioner stands on the other side from the painful ear. If the left ear is hurting (see figure 31 on page 91), he is on the patient's right side. Now the patient gently places his head on the magnetizer's chest. The latter's left hand is lying lightly on the throat between the neck and the back of the hand. The fingertips of the right hand are lightly laid on the painful ear. Here too, the contact must be extremely light.

When laying on the fingers one should always make sure that the strongest emanation takes place through the thumb, the index finger and the middle finger, as we have already seen during the rapport.

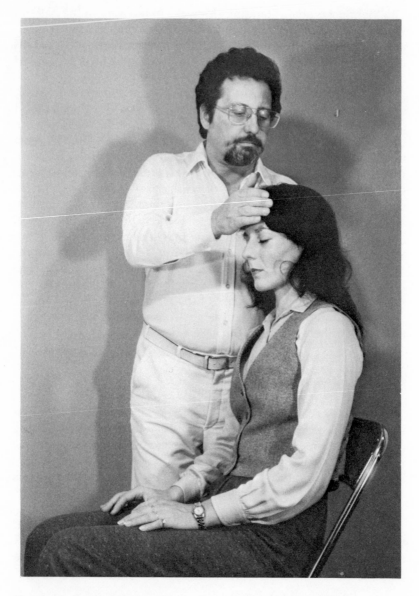

Figure 30. Use a very light touch when stroking the forehead.

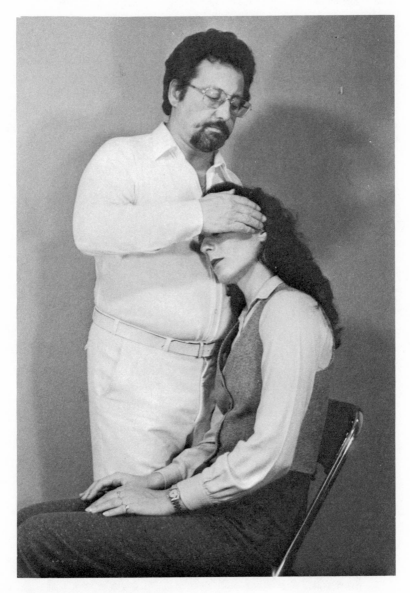

Figure 31. Stroking the left ear.

With the ear strokes you can treat various diseases of the ear, as well as toothache and neuralgia in that region. The duration of treatment is approximately five to seven minutes.

Stroking the Knee

Positive treatment: The patient is seated and relaxed with his hands in his lap. The magnetizer sits opposite. The stroke starts above the knee joint on the outside of the thigh, and continues slowly downward over the joint to about the middle of the tibia. Now bring the hands in a curve going out to the left and right, and bring them back

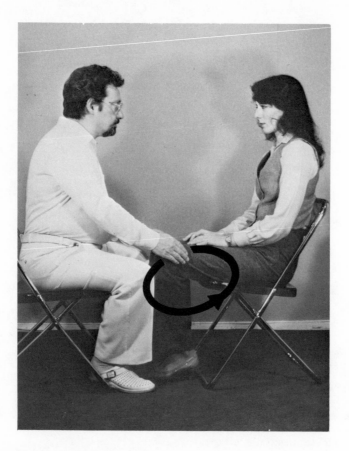

Figure 32. The positive knee stroke.

to the starting point, where you put them down again gently (see figure 32). The positive treatment of the knee is particularly suitable for all the wear and tear this joint undergoes (arthritis, etc.) to bring new energy, and in this way has a rejuvenating effect.

Negative treatment: The starting point for the patient and the practitioner is the same as for the positive treatment, but the patient is not actually touched during this form of treatment. The hands are passed over the joints at a distant of about three to eight inches. The stroke again starts on the side of the joint and continues further down. At the end of the stroke the hands are again moved outwards

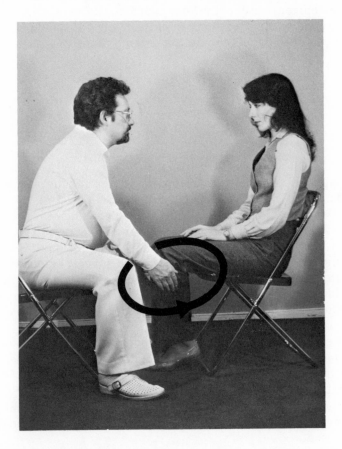

Figure 33. The negative knee stroke.

and are shaken thoroughly, in the normal way for negative treat-ment. The stroke is carried out faster than in the case of positive treatment in order to achieve a drawing off effect.

The flinging movements have already been described in detail in the section "General Negative Treatment." As indicated with the positive stroke for the knee, the hands should also be slightly bent, and with the stroke the fingertips should be directed on the ear, or in this case, on the knee joint to be treated (see figure 33 on page 93).

Clench your hands lightly into a fist before shaking out. Then make a vigorous shaking off movement to the left and to the right, as if you wanted to fling off something that was sticking to your hand.

The negative treatment is very suitable for the treatment of inflammatory diseases of the knee joint like arthritis, sprains, sports injuries and so on. The duration of the treatment should be up to seven minutes, depending on the severity of the case.

Stroking the Heart

The patient is again seated in a relaxed position, and the practitioner stands on his right. The left hand is lightly placed on the right shoulder blade, the right hand on the patient's heart region. For treating the heart, no movement of the hands takes place. Neverthe-less, it is a form of positive treatment. The laying on of the hands over the region of the heart has to be carried out very lightly without any pressure at all. Furthermore, the palms of the hand should not be laid on, but only the fingertips. The hand is therefore held slightly bent. These holds are also called "floating holds" because the treating hand is floating, rather than laid on.

Now concentrate the will strongly on the transference of the vital force. With this hold, again radiate the conviction that you want to help the sick person. The treatment for the heart brings relief to most heart conditions and pectoral complaints (see figure 34). The duration of the treatment should be approximately three to five minutes, twice or three times daily, depending on the gravity of the illness.

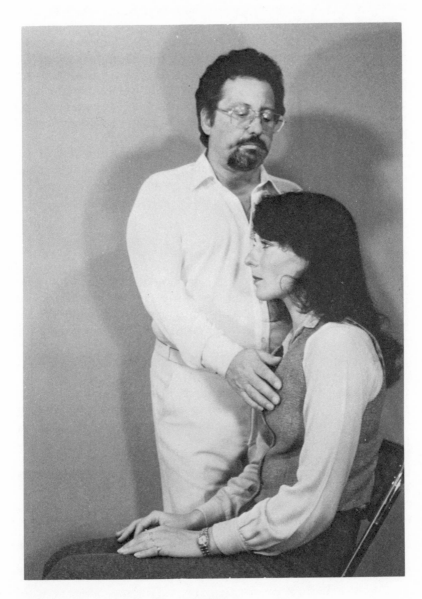

Figure 34. The stroke for heart treatment.

The Stroke for the Stomach

This grip is another floating grip. The patient can be treated seated or standing. The magnetizer stands on the patient's right side. The left hand rests lightly below the patient's right shoulder blade, the right hand is placed on the stomach region. Since the sagittal line runs through the stomach region, the ball of the right hand should be placed on this imaginary line so that about two-thirds of the hand comes to rest on the left side of the patient's body (see figure 35). The treatment is carried out in the same way as the treatment for the heart.

The stomach treatment is indicated for most diseases of the stomach and for malfunctioning of the pancreas. The duration of the treatment should be approximately three to five minutes.

The Laying On of Hands

In a great many cases, this form of treatment, also known as "imposition" in technical jargon, has an extremely beneficial and soothing effect. You can use both hands or work only with the right hand. The decisive factor is which hand you think can give off the most magnetic force.

The laying on of the hand is probably one of the most practiced forms of magnetic healing treatment. It is also frequently carried out without the person who understands it being aware of the implications. This happens particularly when mothers unknowingly place their hand on the forehead of a sick and feverish child to produce a cooling and soothing effect. As in all other magnetic healing manipulations, the law of polarity should be strictly observed during the laying on of hands. Therefore when the magnetizer is standing or sitting in front of the patient, the hand with the opposite polarity should always be placed on the aching spot, i.e., the right hand on the left side and the left hand on the right side (see figure 36 on page 98).

If you are standing behind the patient, you must, of course, cross over so as to maintain the polarity. The laying on of hands

Figure 35. Treating the stomach.

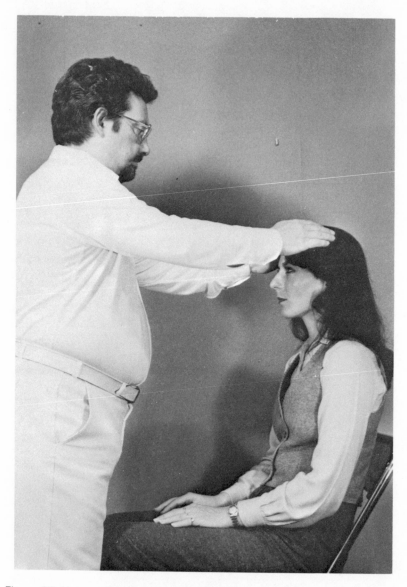

Figure 36. Using opposite polarity when laying on hands.

itself should also be carried out gently and should hardly be felt. It is generally used for treating headaches at the back of the head and as a calming treatment in the care of nervousness and agitation. It can also be used as an additional treatment for the loss of hair. The duration of the treatment should be approximately three to five minutes.

Magnetic Radiation (Pull-outs)

Radiation is particularly effective and suitable for selective localized treatment. The treatment itself is carried out with the right hand, which emits the magnetic radiation. The left hand has the function of forming an opposite pole. The sick part of the body is taken between the two poles.

The right hand is lightly and loosely bent; the fingers are held in such a way that all the fingertips aim at an imaginary point as shown in figure 37 on page 100. The position of the hand is comparable to the feeling produced when you lift a round object with one hand (e.g., a large salt shaker or a bottle). Place the fingertips at about half an inch from the point to be treated, and at the same time concentrate your entire energy on the fingertips of your right hand with the command to radiate a strong magnetic force.

The effect of the radiation should last about twenty to thirty seconds. Then slowly withdraw your right hand, as if you were polling a thick substance from the point of treatment. When the hand is sufficiently far removed, splay out your fingers and shake vigorously.

After this the fingers are bent again in the way we have described and are once more placed near the point of treatment. After thirty seconds, shake out the hands again, etc. Throughout the manipulation the left hand remains still, and should not be moved.

Since the radiation can be aimed at extremely small surfaces, it is used externally for the treatment of wounds, injuries and stresses. Radiation can also achieve good results in the case of internal processes—for instance, with inflammation of the sinus.

The duration of the treatment is approximately five to ten minutes.

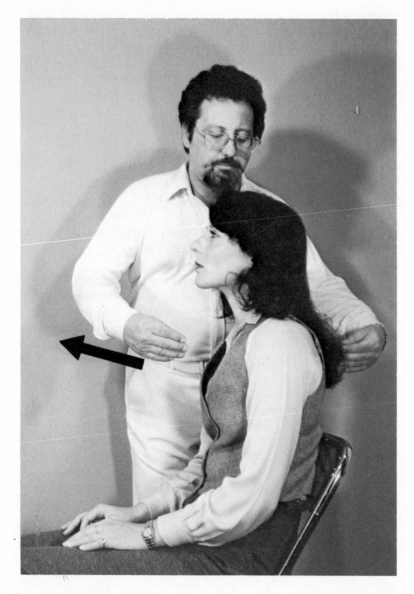

Figure 37. Radiating the heart region. Note the position of the fingers on the right hand. This is the hand that will withdraw the unhealthy energy from the body.

Magnetic Drawing Off

Drawing off painful or sick parts from the body can also be done while the patient is lying down. To do this, hold both hands (hanging down loosely, with fingertips pointing downwards) about three feet vertically above the sick part of the body (see figure 38 on page 102); then lower the hands slowly to about three inches over the body. After that, pull them slowly up again, turn away from the patient and shake the hands energetically. Always make sure the hands do not touch each other.

As with other magnetic healing strokes and holds, it is important that they are carried out in a very relaxed way. There should never be any strain or tension. This manipulation should be carried out about seven to eleven times per session.

Magnetic Water

Older works on healing magnetism repeatedly describe how the old magnetopaths transmitted the magnetic fluid, not only in general and specific treatment, but also to objects and drinks, and sometimes even to food. This served to contribute to healing the sick person and, above all, to have a magnetic effect when the practitioner was no longer present.

Objects necessary for the treatment of wounds were magnetically activated, such as cotton, wool, flannel, oil, and charcoal. In the past it was customary for the magnetizer to give the patient magnetized strips of flannel to bandage his wounds. Furthermore, pieces of clothing or other objects with which the patient came into contact were often treated. Even now magnetic water is used in addition to the general magnetic healing treatment, since the water has the special property of attracting the magnetic fluid particularly strongly and transferring it to those who need it. This cohesive force of the water is actually not surprising, since water is simply the prerequisite for life on our plant. We know for certain that without water no life is possible on earth. This very necessity may well be the decisive factor why water has a number of unique properties.

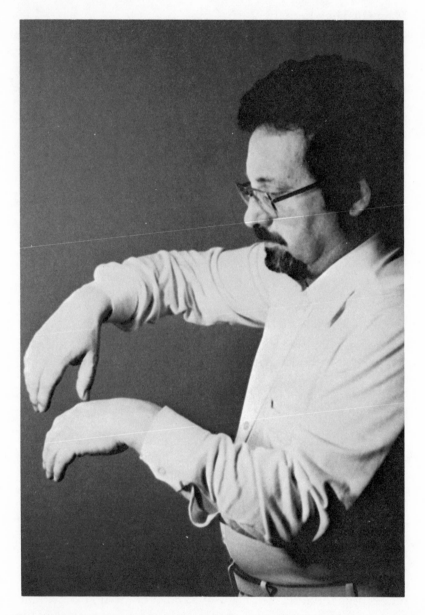

Figure 38. Magnetic drawing off when the patient is lying down.

It may be presupposed that readers understand the basic chemical and mechanical properties of water. This also applies to its electric conductivity, which is possibly connected to the fact that water binds the magnetic fluid particularly strongly to itself. If you consider that the human body consists of 60–70% water and that this water works as a mediator of all chemical and physical processes inside and outside the body cells, this could explain why the transference of vital energy is possible from one human body to another.

Just as water always takes on the surrounding smells, it can be loaded with magnetic fluid. Experiments have shown that in the magnetic field, magnetized water tastes very different from normal water. The radiation of water with colored light has shown similar results. In addition, it has been shown that in both cases the growth of plants could be considerably increased with water treated in this way. (Most plants consist of more than 90% water.) There are numerous other examples showing that water is an ideal medium for the transference of magnetic force, though it is not necessary to mention these here as the interested reader will easily be able to recognize these effects.

Water activated with healing magnetic fluid can be used in a very versatile way for the treatment of various illnesses and painful conditions. Whether it is activated positively or negatively, water is extremely suitable for drinking in the case of internal diseases and illnesses of the digestive organs, as well as for colds and fevers.

Magnetically activated water can also be used for poultices and compresses for swellings, bruises, sprains, and injuries. Its application has been shown to be effective in the case of neuralgic pains and as a gargle for inflammations of the mouth and throat. Obviously it is also possible to bathe parts of the body, or the whole body, in magnetized water.

To produce negatively magnetized water as drinking water or to be used in compresses, take a drinking glass and fill it almost to the brim. Then put the full glass on the palm of your left hand, while the fingers close up round the glass and hold it.

The right hand will now be lightly bent, as we have described in the section on "Radiation." With the fingertips of the right hand you "radiate" onto the surface of the water while concentrating your will to transfer as much as possible of the magnetic force from the fingertips to the water (see figure 39 on page 104). After five to eight

Figure 39. Making negatively magnetized water.

minutes the glass of water may be so strongly enriched with the fluid force that the saturation point has been reached.

To produce positively magnetized water the described procedure is simply carried out with the opposite hand, i.e., the glass is now held in your right hand and the left hand "radiates."

When they drink magnetized water, sick or sensitive people perceive a characteristic smell of steel or sulphur. This smell readily distinguishes magnetized from non-magnetized water. Moreover, people who do not usually like drinking water will drink it eagerly. Even people with weak stomachs can easily tolerate it. One of its characteristics is that even in high summer, magnetized water stays fresher for a longer time. Boiling does not destroy the concentration of the magnetic fluid.

It is important, and an essential prerequisite for the healing effect, that after magnetization the water, or the container in which it is kept, is not touched by any other person than the one for whom it is meant. If another person touches the glass first, the healing effect, the enriched fluid, is transferred to him. The person who drinks after him would only be drinking ordinary water. This rule of reaction also applies to compresses made with magnetized water. No third party should touch the compress. Either the practitioner or the patient should apply it. Some magnetopaths maintain that treatment with magnetized water is not suitable for patients who are too weak to drink by themselves or to put the compress on themselves.

It is also possible to activate bath water with magnetic forces. In this instance the magnetizer puts his left hand on the inside of the bathtub and radiates with the right hand. Thus the water has a negative charge (see figure 40 on page 106). To produce positively charged bath water, the hands are simply changed over, so that your left hand radiates while the right hand works as an antipole.

Negatively charged bath water can also be produced by carrying out rapid, negative strokes over the surface of the water at a distance of about one to three inches, as described in detail in the section "Negative Treatment." The strokes start on the northern end of the bath, where the patient's head will be while bathing, so that he faces south.

For magnetic baths to be effective, it is important that the bathtub is situated, if possible, on the magnetic meridian, i.e., in a north-south direction. Deviations of a maximum of 15 degrees to the west or east are still acceptable, but with larger deviations the effect is no longer guaranteed.

Figure 40. Making negatively magnetized bath water.

Nowadays most bathtubs are permanently fixed so that you cannot change their position. If it is found that a bath has been fitted contrary to the magnetic meridian, there is little point trying to produce magnetic bath water for this bath. Before starting on the magnetic manipulations one should first, with the help of a compass, establish the position of the magnetic meridian line in the patient's home. For general magnetic treatment, some experienced magnetizers consider that it is essential to rearrange the treatment room accordingly.

For the application of magnetic water the rules for the general positive treatment obviously also apply. Positively magnetized water has a strong stimulating (toning up) effect and is recommended for all the illnesses where there is an increased need for energy, for example, debility, malfunction of organs, poor circulation, etc.

Negatively activated water is used in cases where there is a surplus of fluid force. Negative water has a drawing off effect and is therefore indicated in the case of inflammations, feverish illnesses, convulsions, and irritations.

Negative water can also be improved by adding fresh lemon juice or sugar according to taste. This drink is especially refreshing when illness is accompanied by a high temperature. Mineral water can be magnetized too. The patient can drink as much of the negative water as he likes and needs: there are no hard and fast rules in this respect. Positively radiated water should be taken in small mouthfuls every half hour, i.e., about a teaspoonful.

For positively or negatively magnetized compresses, the water should be at about room temperature, and it should certainly not be tap water. The water can be lukewarm if desired and can be put near a heater. Poultices and compresses are beneficial for degenerative arthritic diseases, obvious signs of deterioration, or debilities of the organs where negative poultices have proven themselves valuable for inflamed joints and muscles, wounds and tenseness. The poultice is kept on the place to be treated until it has taken on the temperature of the body. A linen cloth tied to a woolen cloth is best for this (as in swaddling clothes). The positive poultice is changed every two hours, the negative poultice every half hour.

Magnetized baths, whether positive or negative, can be given daily during the period of treatment. The bath temperature should be about 34–37 degrees, depending on what the patient finds most comfortable. Under no circumstances should he try to bathe in water as hot as possible, as this often produces the opposite effect to that desired. At the beginning of the treatment one magnetized bath per day can be taken; later on, two baths per week are sufficient.

The General Magnetic Healing Treatment

True magnetic treatment can be divided into two types of treatment, i.e., "positive" and "negative" treatment. Both these kinds of therapy are carried out using special strokes ("passes") and holds. In addition, there are various additional treatments which you may want to use in special cases.

However, it is important for the beginner to first gain confidence and master all the manipulations we have described, and to be able to use them successfully in treatment. Before the beginner reaches this stage, he will have to practice repeatedly.

PREPARATION FOR TREATMENT

There are a number of factors that need to be considered when you decide to treat someone. First, you have an image to maintain in order to help people feel comfortable. Practical advice is offered regarding the timing of treatments, how to handle clothing, jewelry, etc., as well as discussing the possible disturbing factors that might interrupt your session. Hopefully this section will help you feel more comfortable about starting to work with the magnetic energy. After you have practiced for a while, you will probably develop your own methods of working with people and you will notice that you change your working methods depending on what each individual needs from you.

The Image of the Practitioner

The magnetizer comes in direct contact with the patient so the practitioner's external positive and negative characteristics are easily seen by the patient. One should attach importance to appearance, behavior and personal radiation. The success of the treatment will depend on one's own confidence and conviction regarding the healing process.

The hands are the magnetizer's most important tools. Therefore special attention should be paid to the care of the hands. Fingernails should be clean and not too long. Special care should be taken to ensure that fingernails are smooth and have no cracks which could snag on the patient's clothing. The hands should also be kept supple. The skin should be kept smooth by frequent use of hand cream; cuticles which protrude can also easily be caught on clothing, especially on materials like silk and wool, etc., and should be properly groomed.

For the development of the magnetic forces it is essential to cultivate a natural lifestyle. Social drugs should be avoided as far as possible, since they considerably reduce physical and psychic energy. It is this very energy which the magnetizer requires in order to develop the powerful magnetism which he can then transmit to the sick person.

One should not approach a patient on an empty stomach, since this can lead to bad breath. Easily digestible, odorless meals are particularly appropriate because the therapist should not feel hungry during the treatment. On the other hand, a full stomach makes the practitioner sluggish and clumsy, leading to a loss of suppleness, which he certainly requires in order to remain relaxed during the magnetic session.

The practitioner should not wear any strong smelling aftershave, perfume, or deodorant. A neutral smell of freshness, leading to the impression of cleanliness, is a good way to ensure a pleasant emanation. One should dress decently and discreetly.

Treatment Time

Since we are subject to the laws of nature in the same way as any other form of life on our planet, the magnetic healing treatment should, if possible, take place at the particular time of day when the optimal healing results are achieved. Obviously there are cases when this is impossible. This is mainly the case in emergencies, or when acute illnesses make it important to bring relief to the sick person. For the positive treatment, which has a strengthening character, it is best to choose the morning or pre-noon hours if possible, as the healing magnetic forces are considerably increased at that time of day by the sun.

Any illness or suffering requiring a toning-up should, if possible, be treated magnetically between morning and midday. These illnesses include those that entail a great loss of the Odic force, i.e., any conditions of weakness, acute injuries or those with delayed healing, paralysis, poor circulation, degenerative illnesses, etc. All illnesses requiring negative treatment, i.e., sedation, should be treated in the soothing hours of the evening and night. This treatment is appropriate for conditions of agitation, restlessness, insomnia, feverish illness, etc.

Chronic illnesses and suffering should be treated once a day at the start of the magnetic cure. As recovery begins, the treatment can be undertaken every other day, and with further improvement a magnetic session every third day will be sufficient. This interval should be maintained until a complete cure has been achieved.

Acute illnesses, like high fever, extreme injuries and painful conditions require magnetic treatment at least once a day. In particularly severe cases several treatments a day can be carried out at intervals of two or three hours. The magnetizer decides how often treatment should be undertaken, and it depends above all on the patient's condition and on the seriousness of the illness. A session should not take longer than twenty minutes. It is always better to carry out two sessions of fifteen minutes rather than a single one of thirty minutes.

Make sure that the patient has not eaten immediately before the session. It is best to carry out the magnetization two or three hours after the intake of food or one hour before a meal.

At the end of a magnetic cure it is advisable not to break off treatment suddenly, but to slowly increase the interval between the individual sessions and, at the same time, to shorten the time taken for treatment. In the technical terminology this method is known as "ringing out the treatment." When the cure has been completed, it is advisable to undergo a magnetic session every six months in order to transmit a supportive dose of fluid force to the patient.

The Preliminary Talk

Before treating the patient for the first time, a clarifying talk should take place. One should explain in a quiet and objective way the nature and effect of healing magnetism and the transference of the vital force. It would be totally wrong to ask the patient to believe in a miracle cure.

The patient's attitude and state of mind should determine the words you choose to make him receptive to the healing magnetism. Under no circumstances should you order or allow prescribed medicines to be stopped without authorization, because this could have critical consequences for any sick person. It would be irresponsible and foolish to advise the patient or even influence him in this respect. According to German law (and the law of most countries), drugs can only be prescribed by registered doctors or officially authorized healing practitioners.

Also draw the patient's attention to the fact that only in very rare cases does a spontaneous improvement of the condition occur straightaway after treatment. The fluid force needs time to react. It is quite possible that the first treatment is followed initially by a deterioration of the patient's condition. It can also happen that chronic illnesses are reactivated by the healing magnetic treatment, so that, for instance, pains in organs the patient had felt at some earlier stage and had forgotten in the meantime flare up again.

This phenomenon will not seem at all strange to those familiar with nature healing and the way of thinking of holistic medicine. In homeopathy the initial deterioration in condition shows the experienced therapist that he has chosen the correct remedy and that the desired results will soon be achieved.

In this the ideas of Dr. Samuel Hahnemann, the founder of homeopathy, correspond closely with the thinking of the magnetic healing treatment, for his theory is based on the discovery of Paracelsus, who already declared in his time, "It is the dosage that renders a medicine poisonous or curative." Arndt–Schultz's fundamental biological law is also justified in this context, for it says, "Small stimuli encourage, bigger stimuli accelerate, strong ones hamper and the strongest cripple." Before the first treatment, inform the patient about the possibilities and limitations a magnetic healing treatment can have.

If the patient is able to sit, let him sit comfortably on the treatment chair. During the introductory talk, sit in front of him. Don't fix your gaze on him yet, but simply have a friendly and unrestrained talk. Answer all questions conscientiously but not in too much detail, for that could confuse him. Don't overwhelm the patient with scientific notions and technical expressions, for this can give rise to doubts and anxieties in the anxious patient's mind and diminish any readiness to receive the healing magnetic treatment. If you are confronted by a psychic barrier, you will find it very difficult to achieve healing success. A well carried out introductory talk requires the necessary tact and sensitivity.

There are no easy solutions. In general it may be said that it is better not to confuse friendliness with obvious familiarity, even when you know the patient well. You will have to decide yourself what sort of introductory talk you wish to have with a patient. No one else can make this decision for you.

The Rapport

Before beginning with the magnetic treatment in earnest, i.e., actually working with the patient, you should wash and dry your hands well. Then let your arms dangle freely down for a while, so that the blood can flow into your hands; then quickly and vigorously rub the palms of your hands together until they become white.

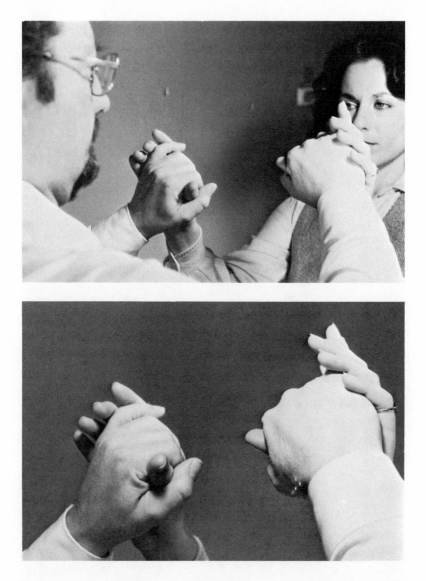

Figure 41. The initial rapport. Top: The patient's left thumb is being held by your right hand, and the patient's right thumb is held by your left. You will now start to fixate the patient. Bottom: A close-up of the position of the hands.

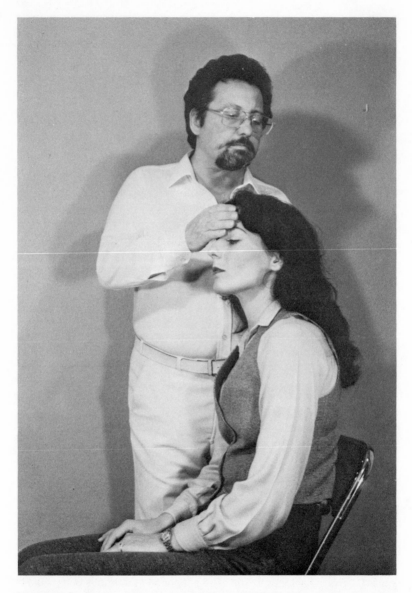

Figure 42. Another type of rapport. Here your left hand is at the base of the head, and the right hand is on the forehead. If you use this technique you cannot begin to fixate until afterward because you cannot look directly at the patient.

(Many magnetizers report that after rubbing their hands together they can immediately notice a slight smell of sulphur, phosphorous or, occasionally, ozone. Finally, stretch out your fingers and shake your hands vigorously.

Make sure that your hands are quite warm. Never treat a patient with cold hands. If you have very cold hands, as is sometimes the case in winter, put them in warm water or over a heater; only then should you touch the sick person.

Before starting with the healing magnetic strokes and holds, you should establish a good rapport with the patient. To do this, stand in front of him, take both his thumbs in your warm hands so that the balls of your thumbs and his are resting on top of each other; at the same time, start "fixating" the patient. Here you should pay attention to the correct polarity, i.e., the patient's left thumb is being held with the right hand and vice-versa. (See figure 41 on page 113.)

You should spend a while in this position until there is a perceptible exchange of heat. This usually happens after one or two minutes. During the rapport you can fixate the patient (as described on page 59).

It is also possible to establish a rapport by laying the hands on the forehead of the patient. Stand to the patient's righthand side. Then put your hands on his neck, the left hand between the neck and the back of the head, and the right hand resting lightly on his forehead. There should also be an exchange of heat at this point. (See figure 42.) In this example the fixation is left out of the rapport. After you have established a rapport, you can start with the general magnetic treatment. At this point you can begin the fixation.

Disturbing Factors

It is not necessary for patients to take off watches, rings, necklaces or any other fashion accessories. Similarly, glasses can be worn quite safely, and coins do not present a problem. Pockets should not be so full that sitting or lying down becomes uncomfortable.

Some of the most disturbing factors during treatment are uncontrollable noises caused, for instance, by the doorbell or the ringing of the telephone. Obviously there should be no television set, radio or record player in the room where therapy is to take place.

Furthermore, there is no need for anyone else to be present in the room during treatment. Relatives of the sick person should be stopped from disturbing the session for any reason. Spectators, even the closest relatives, are a disruptive influence and make it more difficult for the practitioner to concentrate on the patient. Under no circumstances let yourself be talked into having a third person present, even if this person promises solemnly that he will keep very quiet. The mere presence of somebody else acts as a distraction.

This is by no means a secretive or mystical attitude; it is an empirical fact that every magnetizer will confirm. This rule applies in the same way to the presence of animals, especially dogs, cats or birds. The growling of a dog or the mewing of a cat can be very disturbing or distracting, and this jeopardizes the success of the treatment. In my own experience, a canary which was extremely restrained in its song, suddenly burst into such loud, high-pitched chirruping in the middle of a session that I had to interrupt the treatment and could carry on only after the happy singer had been removed.

An ideal treatment room should be quietly situated, neither too light nor too dark. Moreover, the room temperature should be warm enough so that the patient doesn't shiver with cold, as this could lead to uncontrollable muscle movements and tension. Too much heat can be equally disturbing as this could make it difficult for the magnetizer, as the actual magnetic strokes require considerable physical exertion which could make you perspire. Both the magnetizer and the patient should be lightly but comfortably dressed.

Clothing

It is not necessary for the patients to remove their clothes since the vital magnetism penetrates through all natural materials. Bedridden patients can keep on a nightshirt and stay lightly covered up. This does not apply to modern man-made fibers, especially those that produce a lot of static. These materials are easy to recognize because they seem to stick to the body, particularly when the air is very dry. It is advisable for patients to wear clothes made of cotton or natural fibers during treatment.

In this context we should also emphasize the interfering influence of modern carpets. In extreme weather conditions (cold and dry outside with high pressure regions, dehumidifying central heating inside), such strong electric static fields form that even for a healthy person it is very unpleasant to stay in a room with these carpets. Most people have experienced the static discharge and have realized that this is the cause of electric shocks that occur when you touch a door handle or another item of furniture.

If you have your own treatment room, you can bear this fact in mind while planning and furnishing it. Copper or aluminium foil as an underlay for the carpet, as well as an efficient air humidifier, can be very effective. In the patient's home you can only neutralize this charge by using a good humidifier. When it rains, or there is a low pressure area and a sufficient supply of fresh air, nature provides the electrical balance. When the weather is cold and there is a high pressure area, you can use a sprayer like those used for spraying plants, and in this way ensure that there is sufficient moisture in the atmosphere of the treatment room. (You can improve the generally rather sticky atmosphere of the sick room by adding a few drops of peppermint oil to the water spray. In any case it is always a good idea to encourage the patient to provide for sufficient humidity in his rooms after the treatment has finished.)

Position of the Patient

In most cases patients are treated while sitting down. (However, if a patient is seriously ill or weak, he will be treated lying down.) In addition, there are various magnetic holds which are carried out while patients are standing. The magnetizer decides whether treatment should be carried out in a lying or sitting position, depending upon the situation, which varies from case to case. This also depends on whether patients are being treated during a home visit or if the magnetizer has a consulting room.

It is important that patients are relaxed during the treatment. Special care should be taken to ensure that they are not sitting or lying down feeling tense. You should ask them to relax and to slacken all muscles. During the treatment patients can leave their eyes open or shut; there is no hard and fast rule about this. It is only at the beginning of treatment, i.e., at the stage of fixation and rapport, that eyes should be open, though even that is not totally necessary. Particular care should be taken that patients breathe calmly and evenly during the treatment. Before starting with the therapy you should ask them not only to relax, but to breathe in and out deeply.

The Magnetic Meridian

Having determined whether to treat your patient lying down, standing or sitting, it is then important to line the patient up along the magnetic meridian. To do this you need a good compass. When using it you have to be careful that the magnetic needle is not deflected by an interference field. Objects made of iron, steel, or other types of metal with a magnetic effect, as well as various electrical appliances (tv, record player, hot plates, neon tubes, etc.) may have such an influence on the magnetic field of the compass that a precise orientation is no longer possible. Since we are in a constant force field of about 0.5 gauss on this planet, you should always put the patient into the best possible position for treatment.

If the patient is in the wrong position, it can weaken the transference of the vital energy and slow down the healing process, and at worst, render the treatment ineffective. Hence the following rules are of value in preparing the patient:

1. Whether the patient is sitting or standing, he should be facing south, the back of his head turned towards the north.

2. If the patient is lying down, the top of the head should be pointing north, and the feet should be pointing south.

If you have your own treatment room, there should be no problem setting up the couch so that the head of the person to be treated is pointing north. If you use a chair, there should basically be no problem either, since it can also be lined up with the meridian.

There may be problems when you treat a bedridden patient. If the patient's bed is facing east-west, by turning the head sideways (the face to the south) and by turning the body through a few degrees (as far as the width of the bed allows this), it is still possible to find an approximate optimal position for treatment.

Part 3

INSTRUCTIONS
FOR TREATMENT

They shall lay hands on the sick, and they shall recover.

St. Mark 16:18

ADDICTION

Not only young people but people of all ages are nowadays tempted to some extent to consume excessive amounts of stimulating products (alcohol, nicotine, coffee). Others take painkillers at the slightest complaint or indisposition, often more as a "preventive measure" to avoid pain. One of the worst aspects of our time is drug addiction. There are daily reports in the press on the consequences of this evil.

Causes: The causes are usually found in the psychological field with abnormal behavior directed towards the outside world. Social factors play an important part. In adults, stress, pressure to succeed, loneliness, professional demands, troubled relations with family or partner, and sometimes physical ailments (e.g., migraine) are responsible for the increased use of alcoholic drinks, "chain smoking" or constant cups of coffee. Young people, often under eighteen, and sometimes even schoolchildren, are pushed to the use of drugs out of boredom, fear of school, conflict with their parents, or for other reasons. In some cases, dealers systematically force children to become addicted. In all cases the only remedy is a radical cure where drug addiction is concerned.

Symptoms: There is nothing wrong with the moderate consumption of wine, beer, spirits, the "cigarette or cigar to help digestion," or with a stimulating cup of coffee. Furthermore, in acute cases, taking painkillers is perfectly justified. However, anyone who feels constantly compelled to take any of these remedies in excessive quantities, and in larger and larger doses in order to feel comfortable, can be said to suffer from a dependence or an addiction.

The process of addiction usually develops slowly over a prolonged period of time. At first, tiny amounts are no longer sufficient to be stimulating or effective. Without the stimulant the person concerned is nervous, low in performance and shaky. There may be complaints of various kinds, such as nausea, dizziness, tiredness, and headache. In the case of drug addicts, physical and mental decline, loss of appetite, and delusions are common symptoms that can be detected. In addition, the addict endeavors to maintain an apparent state of well-being by taking more and more drugs. In the course of time, the drugs-which may be relatively weak at first—are replaced by stronger ones, and finally hard drugs. The addict will do anything to "get a fix."

Therapy: Healing magnetism can be extremely effective in the initial stages. Every addict requires medical treatment and healing magnetism can only have a supportive effect.

General treatment: Negative therapy. In addition, one may achieve a calming effect by means of imposition and the forehead stroke.

AGITATION

Depending on their disposition, people have different temperaments. Four main types can be distinguished:

Choleric type: Powerful, passionate, hot tempered, easily aroused.

Sanguine type: Easy-going, cheerful, optimistic—though clear and sober.

Melancholic type: Calm, slow, reserved, often pessimistic.

Phlegmatic type: Apathetic and contented, sentimental, cautious.

Choleric types are prone to outbursts of agitation. Usually these fade as quickly as they have arisen. However, if this becomes a permanent condition, the matter should not be taken lightly. The same applies to the sanguine, phlegmatic and melancholic types. If these types suddenly become frequently agitated over trivial matters which normally would not have bothered them very much, this is indicative of a condition of agitation.

Cause: The cause is nearly always stress, extreme professional and personal demands, pressure, and social or domestic maladjustment. In very rare cases the condition is caused by pathological changes in the brain. Basically this is a condition of psychological irritability for which the nervous system can only compensate with unusual outbreaks of temperament.

Symptoms: The choleric type suddenly becomes excited for prolonged periods about things that would not have affected him previously in spite of his temperament. Sanguine types become pessimistic-aggressive; melancholic and phlegmatic types become quarrelsome, obstinate and intolerant.

General treatment: Negative therapy. A special treatment would be the forehead stroke.

Supplementary measures: Walks in the fresh air, physical exercise, and regular work with periods of rest have a supportive effect. Baths in negatively magnetized water will help.

ANGINA PECTORIS

The German word "angst" (fear) dates back to the old German word stem "ang," which is the same as the word "eng" (narrow). In medical use the word "angina" was derived from this word, and it is generally used to describe a constriction. Those expressions which are familiar to the layman, such as angina (referring to inflammations of the throat), and angina pectoris (referring to constriction of the coronary arteries), are only some of the illnesses registered in medicine under the concept of "angina conditions." Angina, as an inflammation of the throat, will not be discussed here, since, in the majority of cases, this is simply an infection. Besides, this form of angina can often appear as a side effect of a dangerous infectious disease, so the doctor should be consulted in any case. A visit to an orthodox practitioner is also a matter of course in the case of angina pectoris, to clarify whether this is a pathological constriction of the coronary vessels or whether it is a "pseudo-angina pectoris."

Cause: In the case of angina pectoris the coronary arteries, which supply the heart with fresh blood, are constricted for organic reasons. As a result of sclerotic processes (for example, deposits on the walls of the arteries) the arteries become blocked to such an extent that the necessary supply of oxygen enriched blood is no longer guaranteed. The lack of oxygen causes the heart muscle to constrict, and the patient experiences pain accompanied by anxiety.

In the case of "pseudo angina pectoris," the coronary arteries contract convulsively as a result of incorrect functioning, though the arteries themselves are quite healthy. This has the same effect. As angina pectoris due to sclerosis is a very serious condition, and healing magnetism can merely play a supportive role, it is important that medical treatment is given at the same time. In serious cases surgical intervention is required. However, in this case healing magnetism can form a valuable and effective additional therapy.

In the case of angina pectoris resulting from a nervous condition, the cause must be sought in the emotional realm where stress, strain or unfavorable influences in the professional or private life of the patient act as important factors in provoking the attack. These tensions may finally result in a heart attack.

Symptoms: Convulsive, contracting pains or stitches in the region of the of the heart, which may radiate to the left, and occasionally also to the right arm; a feeling that the chest is being choked, accompanied by a feeling of panic and annihilation, difficult breathing, and sweating are characteristic symptoms of an angina pectoris attack, which, if left untreated, may finally result in a heart attack. The attack may last for a shorter or longer time, and vary in intensity. Attacks usually occur when the patient is feeling agitated, or they may occur spontaneously shortly afterwards.

General treatment: For angina pectoris resulting from sclerosis use positive treatment; with a nervous condition use negative treatment.

Special treatment: In the case of angina pectoris caused by changes due to sclerosis, use heart therapy; in the case of nervous causes, use the treatment for the forehead and magnetic drawing off in the region of the heart.

Supplementary measures: Nicotine has a particularly unfavorable effect, as does coffee. All excitement should be avoided. If possible, the patient should have regular sleep and exercise in the fresh air. For sclerotic angina, drink positively magnetized water; for the "pseudo" condition, drink negatively magnetized water.

APPETITE, LOSS OF

Appetite refers to the pleasure experienced when eating. While many corpulent people have a good appetite all the time (as opposed to hunger, which expresses the desire of the body for the intake of food), some people suffer from a lack of appetite. If this is only a passing phase, perhaps as the result of overindulgence in food or drink for some reason, or because there is no time to eat, then there is no cause for alarm. However, people who have permanently lost their appetite may lose too much weight. If they are put off by food, especially meat or sausages, these may be alarming signs which should be reported without delay to the doctor or healing practitioner. These symptoms could mask a serious illness.

Cause: Very frequently loss of appetite results from emotional troubles. In the case of an adult, the cause may be high professional demands, domestic conflict, love sickness, or a fear of life. Nowadays even school children can suffer from a sort of "school stress" which may provoke these reactions. Young children may feel neglected, or "mothered" too much, and react by refusing to take food. In adolescents, puberty may play a role. The cause of appetite loss may be an infectious illness which is incubating. In older people, an insufficient production of gastric juices can be responsible for this condition.

Symptoms: When one doesn't feel hungry, when the stomach rumbles and favorite dishes remain untouched, when young children push their plates away, when schoolchildren throw away their break-time snack, and when adults declare that they are full up after the first mouthful, these are signs of loss of appetite.

General treatment: When it has been established that a lack of appetite is based on psychological disorders, the vegetative system should first be calmed. This is done with the negative general treatment.

Special treatment: Positive strokes from the region of the liver to the stomach region.

Supplementary measures: Drink positively magnetized water.

ARTHRITIS, OSTEO-ARTHRITIS

Arthritis (arthrosis deformans) is defined as a degenerative disease of the joints, a condition revealing the wear and tear on the system. The most common form is osteo-arthritis of the knee joint; this may affect one or both knees. Very complex reactions take place inside the knee joint and scientists do not yet agree about the pathological causes.

Cause: The lack of synovial fluid, as well as wear and tear on the cartilage, may cause osteo-arthritis. Frequently the two causes go hand-in-hand. Acute arthritis (arthritis acuta), which develops in early life as a consequence of injury, infectious disease, rheumatic fever, hormone disorders, etc., can also produce osteo-arthritis, as can constant use or the general process of aging. Overweight people suffer from osteo-arthritis more frequently than people of normal weight.

Symptoms: In the case of osteo-arthritis of the knee joint, the patient suffers severe pain when walking and standing up, whereas he feels no pain (or virtually none) when sitting or lying down. It is common to feel the pain when getting up from a resting place; the patient immediately feels an intense pain as he stands up or walks, and this pain only gradually eases and subsides slowly when he rests again. Another typical symptom of osteo-arthritis is the soft "grinding" of the joints when they are moved without any strain.

General treatment: For acute arthritis—negative general treatment, negative knee stroke. For osteo-arthritis—positive general treatment and positive knee stroke.

Supplementary measures: When a patient is overweight, this should be treated as a matter of priority, as indicated in the section on obesity. It is quite possible to combine the two methods of treatment by treating the obesity one week, and the osteo-arthritis the following week, in accordance with the instructions given.

In the case of arthritis acuta, apply poultices with negatively activated water. For arthrosis deformans, poultices with positively magnetized water are recommended in the intervals between treatment.

ASTHMA

Asthma consists of a sudden and unexpected attack of difficulty in breathing. Two main types of asthma can be distinguished: bronchial asthma (asthma bronchiale) and heart asthma (asthma cardiale). In addition to these two main types, there are various other kinds in which the attack is provoked by other illness such as diseases of the liver or kidneys or from diabetes, gout, cerebral sclerosis, etc. Since asthma attacks may also occur in conjunction with fatal illnesses, the doctor should always be consulted and it is inadvisable to treat the condition oneself without knowing the precise cause.

Cause: Bronchial asthma is produced by convulsive contractions of the fine bronchial tubes with a swelling of the mucus membrane and by the secretion of a scanty but tough mucus. Scientists have not yet agreed on the reason for it. Hereditary factors can play a part: children with asthmatic parents often suffer from the same disease. Moreover, some people's oversensitivity to certain irritating substances such as dust, pollen, feathers, animal hair, certain gases or smells, medicines, etc., may provoke an attack, as can eating certain foods or changing climates. The third possibility is an abnormal sensitivity of the nervus vagus, i.e., a form of nervous irritability. This could also be called "nervous asthma."

Cardiac asthma occurs with heart patients. The cause is generally an insufficient functioning of the left ventricle, combined with congestion in the lungs. However, attacks in which the patient is short of breath can also occur when there is a narrowing of the coronary vessels, i.e., in angina pectoris caused by a heart condition.

Symptoms: In the case of bronchial asthma the attack generally happens suddenly, almost out of the blue, frequently as a result of strong emotional agitation. The patient can be frequently surprised by an attack at night while he is asleep. This manifests itself in extreme shortness of breath and feelings of oppression; the patient sits up or opens the window to let in air. The rate of breathing usually increases to double or treble (forty to sixty breaths per minute).

The clearly audible hissing noise when breathing is very characteristic, whereas breathing out is wheezy and heavy, putting a great strain on the stomach muscles. Attacks of a prolonged duration are accompanied by frequent coughing fits which produce a scanty but tough mucus.

Cardiac asthma often develops over a number of years. At first the person is only aware of a feeling of constriction in the chest which increases with physical strain and emotional agitation, and is linked to the beating of the heart. The severe shortness of breath only occurs at an advanced stage, though the hissing noise is breathing in, and labored breathing out, are present from the beginning. In addition, there are symptoms which do not occur with bronchial asthma, such as pains around the heart and under the breast bone, which radiate into the arms. A general fear of death and a rapid and irregular pulse accompany this.

Therapy for bronchial asthma:
   General treatment: Negative.
   Special treatment: Radiation of the chest.

Supplementary measures: If the invalid knows what causes his bronchial asthma, he will avoid contact with the factors which provoke attacks. For asthma caused by the climate, a move to another place to better weather conditions often helps as a last resort. Drink negatively magnetized water.

Therapy for cardiac asthma:
   General treatment: Positive.
   Special treatment: Treatment for the heart.

Supplementary measures: With cardiac asthma, under no circumstances give up medical treatment. Healing magnetism has only a supporting role here. Drink positively magnetized water.

BRONCHITIS

The bronchii are the main tubes of the trachea. Bronchitis (or a bronchial catarrh) is the condition arising when the mucus membrane of these fine tubes is inflamed. The bronchii have the function of protecting the lungs from harmful influences; heavy air pollution is intercepted by the bronchii and is discharged as far as possible by coughing.

Cause: An inflammation or irritation of the bronchii usually results from breathing in harmful substances; nowadays these are mainly environmental toxins, unhealthy air in the work place and the self-imposed smoking of tobacco. Other infections may also cause bronchitis, which in the case of minor symptoms may be associated with an influenza infection, and in more serious cases, with severe illnesses (measles, viral influenza, whooping cough, typhus, etc.). In the case of prolonged bronchitis or coughing, there is a possibility of a bronchial carcinoma (cancer of the trachea). In any case it is absolutely essential to go to the doctor.

Symptoms: Coughing, usually starting with a slight cough in the morning, becoming more frequent and finally chronic. At first the sputum is tough and transparent, becoming increasingly slimy. In addition, breathing is accompanied by rattling, whistling, purring noises (to mention but a few). Chronic bronchitis may also develop without any mucus secretion. The use of healing magnetism should only take place after a doctor or a healing practitioner has been consulted, and after there has been a thorough examination.

General treatment: Positive.

Special treatment: Magnetic radiation in the chest, alternating with positive cross strokes from the back to the shoulderblade region.

Supplementary measures: It is a good idea to spend as much time as possible in the fresh air; smoking and staying in smoky or badly aired rooms should be avoided as far as possible, as should the excessive consumption of alcohol (which has the effect of beating on the back). Warm compresses with positively magnetized water on the chest.

CARDIAC RHYTHM DISTURBANCES

The heartbeat is automatically controlled and orginates in the sinus node, which may be referred to as the natural "heart pacemaker." Electric impulses are transmitted to the heart muscle through the nervous system, resulting in rhythmic heart activity. The contraction of the heart and resulting pumping of blood into the arteries is referred to as the systole; the relaxation is known as the diastole. The normal heartbeat of a healthy adult is about 60 to 80 beats per minute.

The sinus node is linked to the vegetative nervous system, which is independent of our will. In cases where the rhythm of the heart can no longer be maintained naturally, or where the impulses necessary to stimulate the beating of the heart are too irregular or too weak, doctors are using an artificial pacemaker.

Cause: Irregular impulses affecting the nervous system may lead to a premature beat, i.e., extra systoles may arise. Mechanical influences such as pressure, unaccustomed or sudden strain, organic diseases of the heart, injuries, fever, heat, cold, lack of oxygen, and psychological factors (such as agitation, joy, anxiety, anger, sudden changes in the environment, etc.) may cause a change of heartbeat.

An old German proverb states: "The gods have put diagnosis before therapy." This applies especially to the heart and all the pains, troubles and illnesses linked with it.

Symptoms: The patient suddenly "feels" his heart. Without any recognizable or psychological reason, he becomes aware of his heartbeat. Frequently the affected person cannot get off to sleep because his heart suddenly begins to race. He can feel it pulse in his throat. Moreover, the feeling that the heart may "stop" in between beats or "decrease" are signs of disturbances of the heart rhythm, as well as a sign that the pulse is too rapid or too slow. In addition, typical symptoms of bad circulation (paleness, dizziness, outbreaks of sweating, anxiety) may also arise.

General treatment: Negative.

Special treatment: Treatment for the heart.

Supplementary measures: Take baths in negatively activated water before going to sleep.

CARDIAC WEAKNESS

The heart pumps the blood through the veins to the finest capillaries. The blood is responsible for supplying all the vital substances (oxygen, nutrients, vitamins, etc.) for the discharge of harmful waste products of metabolism (carbonic acid, waste materials, etc.), as well as for a number of other processes and protective functions. The heart ascertains that a sufficient amount of blood is present at all the required points and that all of the regions of the body are supplied. In normal circumstances with a healthy heart, four to seven litres of blood are required per minute. An enormous volume of blood is being pumped every day. When someone suffers physical or psychological strain, the volume may increase to thirty litres per minute. It is obvious that the heart's constant performance is absolutely essential for a normal life.

Cause: There may be many causes for a damaged heart, and it is impossible to go into all of them here. Every disease of the heart, as well as all conditions pointing toward a heart problem must be referred to a specialist for precise diagnosis. The heart is subjected to natural ageing processes. Rheumatism of the joints or nicotine abuse can damage the heart and when this is the case, the heart muscle (myocardium) would be most affected.

Symptoms: The symptoms are numerous. The main symptom is a reduction of physical efficiency; the patient becomes short of breath, even with only a slight strain (e.g., climbing the stairs). He has pains of varying intensity in the region of the heart, and swollen legs (oedema). When resting, mainly during the night, the patient has to pass water frequently. Patients suffering from heart disease are usually "digitalized," i.e., the doctor prescribes special drugs (digitalis preparations) to stimulate the heart muscle. Urinary drugs (diuretics) are often prescribed for the increased secretion of water.

General treatment: Positive.

Special treatment: Magnetic radiation of the region of the heart.

Supplementary measures: Medicines should in no case be stopped. Drinking positively magnetized water has a supportive role.

CIRCULATION, DISORDERS OF

The blood has the vital task of providing all organs and cells with oxygen and nutrients to take away accumulated metabolic waste products. The supply of blood takes place by means of the arteries, which split up into increasingly small and fine blood vessels (capillaries). The cells remove the oxygen and nutrients from the blood and discharge carbonic acid and any other waste products. This very complicated chemical-physical process is referred to as metabolism.

The regions of the body furthest removed from the heart (peripheral regions) like the legs, feet, arms and hands are most susceptible to being deprived of sufficient arterial blood; but a low circulation can also become noticeable and increasingly dangerous in other organs which require a great deal of blood, such as the brain and the cardiac vessels.

Causes: Poor circulation in the arms and hands can, in most cases, be explained by a constriction of the supplying arterial veins, which may be caused by too much tension in the nerves. The "calcification" of the walls of the arteries may be the cause of this, especially in older people.

Symptoms: Usually the patient complains of cold hands; often a feeling of numbness or unpleasant tingling in the fingers and finger-tips indicates the supply of blood is insufficient. The patient may have poor circulation in the legs and feet. In mild cases the feet feel cold and there may be a tingling sensation in the toes and on the backs of the feet. At a more advanced stage the person feels intense pain, especially in the tibia and calf. The patient can only walk a short distance without feeling pain, and then has to stand still to let the pain die away. The patient may stand in front of a shop window while recovering or he walks with a limp, described in medical jargon as an intermittent limp (*Claudicatio intermittens*). The expression "smoker's leg" is also a popular description. Undoubtedly nicotin is a decisive factor in this disease. Nevertheless, there are non-smokers who suffer from it. In these cases hereditary causes seem to play a part.

General treatment: Positive.

Special treatment: Local, positive partial strokes over the sick parts of the body, always towards the heart.

Supplementary measures: Absolutely no smoking. Animal fats are to be avoided, whereas vegetable oils high in essential fatty acids are recommended. Take baths in positively magnetized water.

COMMON COLD

The common cold, also called nasal catarrh, is a very widespread complaint from which almost everyone suffers during the course of life. It consists of an inflammation of the mucous membrane of the nose.

Causes: The acute cold is caused by a viral infection. The body is particularly susceptible to colds when it becomes cold and wet, when its defense mechanisms are weakened, as well as after alcohol abuse. Similarly, the effect of dust can also cause nasal catarrh. In the case of a simple cold, only the mucous membrane is inflamed, but in severe cases the sinus (maxillary sinus, frontal sinus, sphenoidal sinus, ethmoid cavity) may be affected and become inflamed as well.

The sinuses are connected to the nasal passages and it is possible for these passages to become blocked when the mucous membrane is badly swollen. This results in pressure in the sinuses. In this case, a doctor should certainly be consulted.

If children catch a cold, it is always advisable to see a pediatrician as many childhood illnesses (measles, whooping cough, etc.) start with catarrh.

Symptoms: Everyone is familiar with the common cold—the runny, red nose and a general feeling of being unwell. If, on top of the viral infection, there is also a bacterial infection, the common catarrh may change into a serious cold. In this case, the nasal secretion is mixed with pus and also with blood.

If the sinuses are affected, they become sensitive and painful when the area is lightly tapped with the finger. The area to test would be above the base of the nose, below the base of the nose on the left and right, around the eyes, as well as to the left and the right sides of the nose.

General treatment: Negative.

Special treatment: Magnetic radiation of the nose and forehead. To finish off the treatment (in order to support the circulation), apply the treatment for about one minute.

Supplementary measures: Mouthsful of negatively magnetized water throughout the day.

CONSTIPATION

Normally we have one bowel movement a day. However, every person is an individual and the intestines are conditioned from very early childhood, so some therapists use the following guideline: it is considered normal to have bowel movements up to three times a day or once every three days. Anything between these two extremes is regarded as being acceptable. Many people, of whom the majority are women, suffer from constipation and are only able to empty the intestines with the regular use of laxatives.

There are two main kinds of constipation: 1) hyperactivity of the intestines because the intestine lacks tone; 2) tenseness of the intestines (spastic constipation). Apart from these two kinds, there are several other kinds of constipation which are based on inadequate functioning or a disease of the digestive organs (for example, in the case of liver disease, hepatic constipation, caused by tumors or inversion of the intestine). If the constipation stretches out over a prolonged period of time, it becomes chronic. Chronic constipation is one of the most common diseases of our civilization.

The diagnosis of constipation should always be left to an authorized therapist, since it is not uncommon for illnesses of the digestive organs to be concealed by an apparent underactivity of the bowels.

Causes: The main reasons for intestinal sluggishness are frequently to be found in poor diet and a sedentary way of life. Because our food is over-refined and denaturized, our intake of roughage is too low. (It consists mainly of cellulose.) Consequently virtually all the food is digested in the small intestine and the little that remains is thickened to such an extent by means of the extraction of water in the large intestine that, on account of the limited volume, there is insufficient activity of the muscles (peristalsis) necessary to move the contents of the intestine forward. The constant use of laxatives (often over years or even decades) frequently produces the opposite effect, i.e., an underactivity of the intestine. Besides, the membrane of the intestine may become so irritated by these that it becomes inflamed. Moreover, the intestinal bacteria (intestinal flora) are likely to be affected.

Spastic constipation results from a tensing up of the intestines, triggered off by psychological disorders, i.e., psychological reasons cause the cramps (spasms).

Symptoms: When underactivity of the intestine is the problem, the patient has bowel movements only at great intervals, and can only empty the bowels with considerable effort involving pain. The stomach is hard and tense, usually sensitive to pressure. Furthermore, there is a loss of appetite, bad breath (halitosis), and the tongue has an unpleasant coating. Tiredness and headaches are very common. These symptoms usually fade after a bowel movement.

When one has spastic constipation, the patient feels as if the intestines were contracting, and he also feels full and sometimes has colicky abdominal pains. The excreted contents of the intestine are in the shape of small pellets ("sheep's droppings") and seem dried out and compressed.

Therapy: Healing magnetism only has a supportive function in curing constipation. The patient should gradually reduce the amount of laxatives and eat a healthy diet rich in roughage. Raw sauerkraut, fresh vegetables, salads, wholemeal bread, and curdled milk are recommended. In addition, soaked dried plums or figs, as well as a teaspoonful of linseed, have a laxative effect.

General treatment: For hyperactivity of the intestine—positive.

Special treatment: The left hand rests on the back around the sacrum; the right hand carries out circular positive strokes clockwise around the navel, including the epigastrium and the hypogastrium.

Supplementary measures: Plenty of exercise in the fresh air, a diet rich in roughage, drink positively magnetized water.

General treatment: For spastic constipation—negative.

Special treatment: The left hand rests on the back, as high up as the sacrum; the right hand carries out circular negative strokes around the navel, including the epigastrium and the hypogastrium. The strokes start off on the median line at the height of the stomach. After each full circle, coming back to the starting point, the hand is slowly pulled away, as though pulling something away. Once the hand is far enough removed from the body, shake it thoroughly, and bring it back in a curve to the starting position and repeat the manipulation several times.

Supplementary measures: Plenty of exercise in the fresh air, a diet rich in roughage. Before going to bed, drink half a glassful of negatively magnetized water; every other day take a negatively activated, not too hot, full bath.

DEPRESSION

Depression in the psychiatric sense refers to a mood of dejection and sadness. Two types of depression can be distinguished: endogenous depression, arising from inner causes, and exogenous depression, which is provoked by external circumstances. Increasing numbers of people in our society are affected by melancholia and dejection. It is estimated that about 30 percent of all illnesses are of depressive origin. Loneliness and isolation afflict many people in our materially oriented consumer society and many individuals find it difficult to establish contact which creates the ideal climate for the syndrome of depression. The numerous suicide attempts, mostly among the population of the industrial nations, are symptomatic, and demonstrate the despair which can result from depression.

Cause: Endogenous depression is a hereditary condition. Since healing magnetism can achieve little in this instance, we will not dwell on it further. Metabolic, cerebral changes may lie at the root of exogenous depression, i.e., depression is caused by external circumstances or it is self-imposed, according to recent scientific examinations. Thus the condition could be described as a cerebral, metabolic disorder (in the clinical sense). However, each person should always be considered as an entity, so that these considerations have only an analytic or diagnostic relevance.

Symptoms: The symptoms may be many and various, which is why depression is referred to as a depressive syndrome. A syndrome means that there are several simultaneous symptoms. It is particularly because depression frequently hides behind other symptoms (such as constipation, diarrhea, headaches, stomach troubles, insomnia, feelings of guilt, etc.) that the term masked (hidden) depression is often used. Everyone sometimes feels dejected, discouraged and disgruntled. In a normal person these conditions quickly pass. In the event of prolonged symptoms of this kind, an exact diagnosis should be obtained.

General treatment: Positive. The treatment should start by cheering up the patient.

Special treatment: Forehead stroke, following by the laying on of both hands on the head.

Supplementary measures: Contact with other people should not be avoided under any circumstances, but one should try to distract oneself as much as possible. However, a distinction should be made between distraction and excitement. It is not advisable for people suffering from depression to attend many sad events, since their general mood will be adversely affected. Baths with positively activated water have a supportive effect.

EAR INFECTIONS

Children and adolescents frequently complain of earache. Sometimes the pains are related to growth and disappear after a few hours. However, there may be an inflammation of the auditory canal which can sometimes spread to the eardrum. That is why all earaches should be treated by a specialist. Depending where the inflammation is located, the earache is described as a middle ear infection (otitis media), or an infection of the outer auditory canal (otitis externa).

Causes: Ear infections frequently occur as complications in the case of infectious diseases (for example, in the case of diphtheria). Colds and influenza can also be accompanied by an ear infection. Very frequently bad teeth affect the area around the ears, so that they also feel the pain.

Symptoms: The symptoms of an acute middle ear infection include intensely painful earache, as well as headaches and fever, sometimes combined with vomiting. The hearing can be weakened. The area surrounding the ear looks red and feels hot to the touch, at least in the advanced stages. The doctor can recognize the illness by the characteristic change in the eardrum.

Therapy: In the acute condition, as a supportive measure to medical treatment, after discussion with the doctor or the healing practitioner.

General treatment: Negative.

Special treatment: Put both hands lightly on the ears, move them slowly outwards, shake the hands thoroughly, and in a curve, bring them back to the starting position. Carry out this manipulation about nine to eleven times per treatment. When the acute condition has eased off a little, apply the stroke about three times a week for three to five minutes.

EXAM NERVES

Psychologically healthy people, even those with high I.Q.'s, may suffer from a sudden fear of failure before tests and exams, particularly when the result is decisive to their further career.

Cause: In most cases this feeling indicates a predisposition to a highly sensitive character. In the case of children and adolescents, excessively high expectations may lead to exam nerves. The examiner or members of the examining board may sometimes provoke a state of anxiety in the candidate taking the exam, even before it has started.

Symptoms: A few days before the exam the candidate suffers from lack of concentration, and occasionally even loss of appetite. A subject that was thoroughly learned by heart is suddenly forgotten. Suddenly the most simple and logical things cannot be remembered. It is as though one had not learned anything. The fewer questions one can answer during the exam, the worse the condition becomes. The throat feels constricted and one cannot utter a word. Women usually start to cry.

General treatment: Three or four days before the exam, give a daily negative treatment.

Special treatment: Imposition. The laying on of hands over the head, followed by the forehead stroke for about one minute.

Supplementary measures: It makes sense not to go through any subject the day before the exam since nothing will be gained by that. On the contrary, excessive preparation will act only as a further strain on the nerves, without the brain taking in anything of importance. On the evening before the exam a not too hot, full bath with negatively magnetized water will bring additional relaxation.

FLATULENCE

The food and liquid that we ingest is broken down in the body in the digestive process, i.e., before the organism can utilize the food, regardless of its consistency, it must be more or less broken up into its molecular components, depending on the composition of the solid or liquid food. The digestive juices (enzymes or so-called "ferments") carry out this process, and the chyme produced by chewing passes through the body via various passageways (mouth, stomach, duodenum, small intestine, etc.).

Cause: The food in the mouth may be insufficiently broken down (bad teeth, false teeth) or it may have been eaten too hurriedly (swallowing a lot of air), but in addition, there may be organic illnesses of the digestive organs (stomach, liver, pancreas, small or large intestine), as well as malfunctions of these organs, often caused by incorrect nervous functions which are responsible for the fact that in specific areas the digestive juices secreted are too few or too weak. When consumed in large quantities, food causing intense flatulence (such as cabbage, peas, beans, and fruits) may also make too many demands on the potential of the existing enzymes. Moreover, with increasing age, the natural production of the enzymes is reduced because of a weaker performance of the glands. A diagnosis is therefore essential.

Symptoms: The symptoms are well-known: frequent burping or unpleasant accumulation of air in the intestines, which often causes stomach pains and wind. This can be so extreme that the stomach is distended and the accumulated intestinal gases cause pain (meteorism).

General treatment: Start by treating the basic cause. Positive general treatment works for the symptoms.

Special treatment: Slow, positive strokes from the stomach region to the hypogastrium.

Supplementary measures: Avoid food causing excessive flatulence; chew food thoroughly with plenty of saliva. Drink positively activated water.

FORGETFULNESS, LACK OF CONCENTRATION

It is not only elderly people who tend to be forgetful or who can no longer concentrate properly. People in the middle of their professional lives, and even schoolchildren, frequently complain of not being able to concentrate or remember as well as they need to.

Cause: In the case of elderly people the brain functions become less efficient. At an advanced age sclerosis may reduce the necessary supply of blood to the brain. With younger people, especially when they are under stress, the subconscious often fights off excessive demands. On the other hand, stress and overtaxing may also lead to a state of mental exhaustion, which then becomes apparent, not only as a physical, but also as a mental inefficiency. A visit to the doctor or to the healing practitioner will clarify the matter.

Symptoms: Elderly and old people frequently forget events that have happened recently, whereas they can remember earlier events, going as far back as childhood or adolescence, in detail. Younger people and growing children who have not yet learned to control their thought processes may give the impression that the poor concentration, forgetfulness and the reduction of mental efficiency arise from a conscious defensive attitude or indifference.

General treatment: Positive.

Special treatment: Treatment for the heart, followed by a short radiation of the forehead.

GOITRE

The thyroid gland is a vital hormone producing organ in the human body. The hormones it releases into the blood as required (such as thyroxin) are essential for metabolism, growth of the bones, regulation of circulation, body weight and other functions. An overactive (or underactive) thyroid gland may have serious consequences. The thyroid gland gets its name because it is shield shaped (in German: "schilddruse") in front of the upper end of the windpipe and the larynx.

The complexity of this organ, its many interactions with other organs, and how it is often linked to various malfunctions and illnesses cannot be described in detail here. Therefore we shall only discuss one particularly troublesome, and above all, cosmetically ugly manifestation of a disease of the thyroid: goitre.

Causes: The best known form of goitre is probably caused by a lack of iodine. The precise reason for the enlargement of the thyroid gland may only be established by a doctor, based on detailed examinations and check-ups. Any enlargement requires a medical examination.

Symptoms: Pressure in the larynx and in the front area of the throat, as well as a visible thickening in this part, difficulties in swallowing, and feelings of tightness, may indicate a disease of the thyroid gland, as can losing weight, nervousness, shaking of the hands, protruding eyes and other symptoms.

General treatment: If it is a case of a harmless enlargement of the thyroid gland, as established by a doctor, negative general treatment can be given.

Special treatment: Localized, negative partial strokes from the cheeks over the thyroid gland, and the lateral area of the throat to the collar bone. There, shake out the hand and bring back the hands to the starting point.

Supplementary measures: Use table salt containing iodine. Drink negatively magnetized water.

HEADACHES/MIGRAINE

One of the most common illnesses of our time is migraine. Millions of painkilling tablets are swallowed by people every year. The time taken off work by both workers and employers because of migraine is equally considerable. Even schoolchildren can be the victims of headaches. Migraine makes no distinction between males and females, although a higher percentage of women suffer from it.

Cause: The cause of migraine is still not fully known. It is supposedly a kind of vascular cramp, provoked by the incorrect functioning of the vascular nerves of the head. Naturally many other causes may provoke headaches. Tension in the region of the shoulder and the neck, or changes in the vertebral column are also frequently responsible for the pains. A precise diagnosis is therefore important because diseased organs can also cause headaches. In this case the basic illness must obviously be treated as well.

Symptoms: The thumping, pounding pain occurs like an attack, and may last for hours, or sometimes even for days. Only one half of the head is usually affected. The pain is often accompanied by an aversion to light, nausea, flickering before the eyes and visual disturbances. Strangely, the pains also occur frequently on Sundays and holidays.

There are many reasons which can trigger off an attack: changes in the climate, weather, smells and travelling are as likely to cause a migraine as stress, anger and overwork, etc. In most cases the person concerned does not know the reason for the attack.

General treatment: Negative.

Special treatment: Forehead stroke, eye stroke, depending on the center of the pain.

Supplementary measures: The skillful carrying out of neural therapy (looking for the field of disturbance, selective procain injections), as well as other homeopathic sinus treatments, often produces amazing results. A very soothing effect can be obtained by placing cool compresses, dampened with negatively magnetized water, on the forehead and the eyes.

HIGH BLOOD PRESSURE/HYPERTENSION

Blood pressure is a so-called "operational pressure," and therefore varies from individual to individual. A distinction can be made between the systolic (upper level) and the diastolic (lower level) blood pressure. During the systole the heart muscle is contracted and pushes the blood through the body. During the diastole the heart relaxes and fills up with fresh blood. The pressure, still existing at this phase of the heartbeat, is called the diastolic pressure. The elasticity and the penetrability of the blood vessels, as well as the pumping performance of the heart, play an important part here. The blood pressure level is also abbreviated to "RR," after the Italian, Riva-Rocci, who was the first to invent an easy method of measuring blood pressure.

Cause: Apart from the various organic illnesses (heart, arteries, renal diseases), there is also the case of simple high blood pressure, i.e., the blood pressure rises without any recognizable cause. Anger and excitement may also cause a rise in blood pressure. Only an authorized therapist can establish the precise cause. Therefore it must first be treated.

Symptoms: An extremely red face, and protruding veins on the forehead, usually accompanied by being short of breath, are the external signs that the patient is suffering from high blood pressure. In addition, he may suffer from headaches. Measuring the RR levels will give the required information. The formula: age (number of years) plus 100, gives the approximate average level for the upper limit of the blood pressure. If this average level is exceeded by more than 20 points for a prolonged period, this can be considered to indicate hypertension. (The observation of the lower level of the blood pressure is equally important to the therapist, since this leads to conclusions relating to diseases of other organs, such as the kidneys.)

General treatment: Negative.

Special treatment: Forehead strokes.

Supplementary measures: Instructions for the treatment depend on the diagnosis. In all cases nicotine and alcohol should be avoided. If the kidneys are involved, a low salt diet is recommended. Magnetic radiation in the region of the kidneys is also effective. Drink negatively magnetized water.

HYPERTENSION

Nowadays not only working people suffer from hypertension and irritability, but housewives, schoolchildren and retired people also complain of this. The condition can persist even on days off from work, on weekends, during vacations, or on holiday. Occasionally touchiness manifests itself especially strongly at these times. The number of sedatives taken by these people per year is quite frightening. The constant use of these drugs leads to addiction. In the case of the constant use of some of the drugs, damage to the organs may also occur.

Causes: The balance between phases of activity and rest is disturbed; this means that the body can no longer recuperate sufficiently through sleep or rest breaks to provide a new potential of energy and to calm the nervous system. The main causes for hypertension are irritability, stress, strain and pressure, especially in the intellectual field; but professional or domestic differences or the feeling of "not being understood" may also be responsible.

Symptoms: When otherwise sensible people suddenly worry about trivial matters, when previously compatible husbands and wives quarrel at the slightest provocation, when children behave in a stubborn or aggressive way, when peaceful pensioners start to moan, when colleagues at work suddenly become cantankerous and when employers become irritable and unapproachable, these are often signs of hypertension.

Therapy: The symptoms of a strained nervous system can be treated by healing magnetism.

General treatment: Negative.

Special treatment: Put both hands on the scalp. Follow this by stroking the eye for about one minute.

Supplementary measures: Take a full, negatively magnetized bath before going to bed.

INSOMNIA

Sleep is necessary for recuperation of the body. During sleep conscious and voluntary movement slows down or stops. Strictly speaking, sleep represents a kind of protective mechanism of the body, which fulfills the purpose of renewing the physical energy which has been used up during the day. A huge number of people of both sexes and of many different nationalities suffer from disturbed sleep; billions of sleeping tablets are swallowed every year all over the world. A distinction can be made between problems with getting off to sleep and disturbed sleep.

Causes: The rhythm of sleeping and waking is controlled by the midbrain area—difficulties in going off to sleep may be caused directly by an illness of the midbrain, or indirectly by disturbances from the outside (light, noise, bad smells), as well as by disturbing factors related to the body itself (worries, anxiety, stress, fear, pain, etc.). Too much food eaten before going to bed, or the abuse of nicotine, may also lead to disturbed sleep, as can psychological illnesses (depression) and poor hormonal regulation (menopause, etc.).

Problems with sleeping through the night, i.e., waking up too early, are especially common with older people. The average need for sleep for an adult is about eight hours and decreases with age.

Symptoms: At some time or another, nearly everybody has difficulty getting to sleep, either from excitement (anticipation of a joyful event, travelling plans), or because of sadness and worry. That is normal and very natural. However, anyone who tosses about for hours every night and who remains wide awake and unable to sleep, even after counting an infinite number of sheep, is not affected by a normal sleeplessness: he is suffering from real insomnia.

In the case of problems with sleeping through the night, one may wake up a short time after going off to sleep and find it difficult to get back to sleep again.

Therapy: The main task of healing magnetism consists of stimulating the vegetative nervous system and of re-establishing the natural sleeping pattern.

General treatment: Negative.

Special treatment: Negative strokes from the head over the forehead, and the eyes, along both mammillary lines, down to the region of the stomach. After a treatment lasting ten minutes, have a break of about five to eight minutes and repeat the treatment once more.

Supplementary measures: Before going to bed drink half a glass of negatively magnetized water; every other day take a full, not too hot bath with negatively magnetized water.

Note: It is never a good idea to take sleeping pills for any length of time. In the first place, sleep induced by pills never has the same recuperative effect as natural sleep. (One may "sleep," but the next morning one feels tired, not refreshed as after a good night's sleep.) Secondly, taking strong chemical remedies, especially over a long period without any control, can produce harmful effects and even cause damage to the organs.

KIDNEY/BLADDER DISEASES

The kidneys may be described as highly effective filters in the human body, the perfect functioning of which is of decisive importance to the normal course of all the life processes. The failure of both kidneys inevitably leads to death, since the accumulated metabolic products and other substances which should be discharged can no longer be secreted. The body is poisoned from the inside. Only kidney machines have made it possible to save patients with kidney failure or who have had both kidneys surgically removed (hemodialysis). That is why it is absolutely necessary to consult a specialist (a urologist) at the slightest sign of a disease of the bladder or the kidneys. Diseased kidneys are an extremely serious matter.

Causes: Infections, heart conditions, arteriosclerosis, diabetes, chronic inflammations, poisoning injuries, tumors, kidney stones (to mention but a few of the causes), can all lead to damage of the kidneys, and to illnesses of the bladder, urethra, urinal passage or prostate (if the inflammation or infection spreads).

Symptoms: Pain or a burning sensation when passing water, blood in the urine, the frequent urge to pass water, pressure in the region of the kidneys or unspecified pains in the back, weakness, constant thirst or a prolonged and ongoing state of dizziness, mean that the kidneys should be thoroughly examined. While carrying out the routine analysis of the blood in the laboratory, the doctor frequently comes across otherwise hidden blood, bacteria, protein or sugar. In those instances the doctor will order further examinations so as to establish the precise diagnosis.

All the illnesses of the kidneys or the bladder, as well as of the related organs, must be treated by a specialist. In principle, the basic complaint has to be treated; this also applies to healing magnetic treatment.

General treatment: Positive.

Special treatment: Localized partial treatment of the kidney region with the hands crossed over, then radiate the area of the bladder magnetically with the right hand for about one minute, approximately the width of the hand below the navel. At the same time, the left hand is held over the region of the sacrum.

Supplementary measures: Drink large amounts of positively magnetized water (at least two to three gallons) at intervals during the day. Warm compresses with the same water placed on the area of the kidneys and the bladder have a supportive effect.

LIVER/GALLBLADDER DISORDERS

The liver is the most important central organ of our body and can be compared to a chemical factory. If one wished to recreate artificially all the substances produced and changed chemically by the liver, which are always available simultaneously, then a huge chemical plant of unimaginable dimensions would be required. The bile produced by the liver is of great importance, since bile is the decisive factor for breaking up the fats contained in food and for the detoxification of harmful substances in the body. On average the liver produces about 750 ccm. of bile a day, which is thickened and stored in the gallbladder and released into the duodenum during the digestive process.

Causes: Apart from an inborn weakness of the liver cells forming the bile, the main causes of strain on the liver are a bad diet and environmental toxins (especially the excessive consumption of alcohol and food with an excessively high fat content, the unchecked taking of tablets, etc.). Furthermore, psychological influences may play a part and lead to a diseased gallbladder. As a result of the deposit of certain substances in the thickened bile, gallstones may form, which can also result in great suffering.

Symptoms: Unfortunately the liver does not immediately announce that it is diseased through pain. Frequently only unspecified complaints, such as pressure in the upper part of the abdomen, loss of appetite, flatulence, and diarrhea alternating with constipation, point to a disease of the liver. Persistent tiredness and even headaches may be caused by a disease of the liver. The acute symptoms are nausea, light colored stools, brown urine, yellowish eyeballs, and in the final stage, the yellow coloring of the skin (jaundice = icterus).

In the case of cystic colics, produced by gallstones or inflammation of the gallbladder, there may be convulsive pains in the right upper part of the abdomen, which may radiate to the back and to the shoulder blade. Frequently there is also a sensitivity to pressure in the middle of the right eyebrow. With any acute symptoms it is essential to consult a doctor immediately.

Therapy: During the course of the attack: magnetic discharge to be carried out on the patient, who is lying down. Hold the hands about three feet away from the liver area, lower them, slowly raise them and shake thoroughly.

Additional general treatment: Negative, in case of chronic diseases of the liver and gallbladder.

General treatment: Positive.

Special treatment: The magnetizer's left hand lies on the patient's back; the right hand carries out slow, positive strokes towards the areas of the liver and the stomach. This is followed by magnetic radiation in the region of the liver.

Supplementary measures: Dietary instruction should be followed without fail. Fatty foods and food that is difficult to digest should be avoided, as well as alcohol; moreover, the state of the liver should be checked from time to time. (Get a blood test from a laboratory.) Drinking positively magnetized water has a supportive effect.

LOW BLOOD PRESSURE/HYPOTENSION

The term "hypertension" is often heard nowadays. Low blood pressure, or "hypotension," is also very common, though the term is less well-known. Compared with hypertension, low blood pressure causes less severe damage to the organs. Nevertheless, it is an unpleasant condition which can often have a very disturbing effect on the patient's general well being. People of all ages and both sexes can suffer from low blood pressure. In addition, it affects people with very different constitutions.

Cause: A lowering of the blood pressure can result from a loss of blood following injuries, or because of internal bleeding caused by illness (for instance, bleeding in the stomach from burst ulcers), a weak heart, a heart attack, diseases of the brain or of the hormone producing glands (hypophysis or adrenal glands), but also as a result of shock caused by accident (collapse). Hypotension may also occur with feverish illnesses, during pregnancy, after a serious illness, as a result of a prolonged confinement in bed, as well as with serious disease of the central nervous system.

Very frequently low blood pressure is found in people who are organically completely healthy. In this case it is usually a slackening of the vascular nerves, the causes of which should be looked for in a weakness of the vascular system or in psychological troubles which cause a dilation of the arteries.

When the upper level of the blood pressure falls below 100 mm/hg, this indicates hypotension. It is very important to diagnose the condition precisely, and this can only be done by a specialist. For this reason we shall only deal here with low blood pressure of a nervous or constitutional origin.

Symptoms: People with poor circulation often have a dizzy spell in the morning when they get up, and this is frequently accompanied by listlessness, and sometimes by nausea or sickness. Moreover, it is difficult to get going, i.e., it takes a while for the body to reach its usual level of performance. These symptoms also frequently occur after meals (digestive tiredness). People with poor circulation are especially affected.

Therapy: If there is an organic cause, this should be treated first.

General treatment: Positive.

Special treatment: Treatment for the heart, followed by putting the hands on the top of the patient's head for one minute.

Supplementary measures: Plenty of exercise in the fresh air, a light diet rich in vitamins, airy clothing and regulated activity have a very supportive effect. Baths in positively magnetized water.

MENOPAUSE

The menopause in women is the transition period from full sexual maturity, when the woman is capable of bearing children, to the time when she can no longer do so. In general, this happens between the age of 48 and 52. In exceptional cases the menopause may occur earlier. The age of 43 has been set as the bottom limit (climacteric praecox).

Whereas the female menopause is well-known, it is less well-known that men experience it as well. In medical terms it is known as climacteric virile. The symptoms are certainly not as aggravated as in the female body, nor are they linked to a particular age. Women very rarely give birth after the age of 42. However, a large number of men are fully fertile at a fairly advanced age, sometimes even over 70.

Causes: In women the menopause results from the change in the hormonal production of the body. Too little estrogen is produced. This deficiency of hormones either directly or indirectly triggers off disturbances in the vegetative nervous system in the midbrain area, and this results in poor control. This is self-evident, as a balanced level of hormones is required for the smooth interaction of all the organs and bodily functions.

In the case of the male, there are "change of life" problems when the balance of testosterone and androgen hormones fluctuates too much.

Symptoms: Irregularities in menstruation. The first signs of the female menopause are usually prolonged and heavy bleeding during menstruation, or often only very slight bleeding at irregular intervals. In addition, there are hot flushes, cold shudders, outbursts of sweating, dizziness, loss of sleep, strong changes of mood, low performance often accompanied by occasional depression; irritability is another characteristic side-effect of the female menopause.

In the male menopause the physical and mental performance slows down, and this is often accompanied by palpitations, states of anxiety, nervousness and hot flushes. In addition, the sexual drive and potency are reduced.

Obviously in principle a doctor can always be consulted. Moreover, regular preventative check-ups should be carried out.

Therapy: The prescribed medical therapy can be effectively supported by healing magnetism.

General treatment: Positive.

Special treatment: Imposition for calming down. The left hand is placed on the sacrum, the right hand on the hypogastrium. To finish the treatment, forehead stroke for about one minute.

NECK PAINS

Professional people with a sedentary occupation often suffer from this affliction. However, people who work continuously standing up with one side of the trunk bent over may also suffer from this. Pain in the neck (cervical vertebra syndrome) is included in the group of rheumatic complaints.

Causes: In mild cases of permanent severe strain, the throat and the neck muscles tighten and become hard and tense. In this case there is a muscular tightness. The nerves become tense and this results in pain. At a more advanced stage there may be changes in the cervical section of the vertebral column itself. The invertebral rings (discs) lying in between the individual vertebrae lose their elasticity; they become brittle and bulge out (disc prolapse). Thus pressure on the ends of the nerves may arise, which naturally leads to intense pain. Therefore an X-ray should be made by a doctor so that potential damage to the vertebral column can be detected at an early stage and be treated.

Symptoms: At first the patient feels a stiffness in the neck and any movement is painful to some extent. The muscles feel quite hard. As the illness progresses, the pain radiates to the shoulder area. This is frequently accompanied by headaches. Tenseness in the neck region or damage to the cervical section of the vertebral column are often primarily responsible for migraine (cervical migraine).

General treatment: Positive.

Special treatment: Slow, positive strokes with the hands crossed over, carried out on the patient when he is standing up, from the shoulder blade region to the neck area. At that point, lift your hands away from the body and bring them back in a curve to the starting point, and repeat the manipulation several times.

Supplementary measures: Warm to hot compresses, dampened with positively activated water should be applied to the shoulder and the neck. Leave the compresses for about twenty minutes. Three to four compresses per day.

NERVE STRENGTHENING

Like the organs of the body, the nervous system requires a certain amount of care, since most of the physiological processes of the organism are regulated by the nervous system. Healing magnetism is extremely appropriate for strengthening the nerves and as a preventive measure.

General treatment: Positive.

Special treatment: Alternating stomach stroke, eye stroke, and forehead stroke (with the addition of a special stroke for positive general treatment). On getting up, take a bath with positively magnetized water three times a week.

OBESITY/ADIPOSITY

In this context a distinction can be made between two main types: endogenous obesity (endogenous means originating from within the body) and exogenous obesity, i.e., resulting from external factors.

Endogenous obesity is not as common as is generally thought. Most overweight people suffer from an "eating obsession." Only the therapist, doctor, or healing practitioner can establish the sort of obesity concerned in each individual case. Before the start of healing magnetic treatment an authorized medical person should be consulted.

Cause: The origin of obesity represents a very complex problem; both physical and psychological factors play a part. Frequently these factors are interrelated so that a precise demarcation of the true cause is be no means easy.

There are people who can eat as much as they like without gaining weight. There are others for whom each additional intake of food—each little "nibble"—immediately leads to an increase in weight.

In the case of endogenous adiposity there is usually a disturbance or a malfunctioning of some excretory gland (thyroid, pituitary) and a consequent imbalance of hormones. Since the treatment of these special malfunctions of the glands may only be undertaken by a specialist, we will not go into further details here.

Exogenous adiposity is extremely common nowadays. The main cause is the excessive intake of food high in calories, the copious consumption of spirits and alcoholic drinks, insufficient physical exercise (a sedentary way of life) and the resulting unnaturally long hours of sleep.

Moreover, with many people these days, psychological problems are responsible (being misunderstood, overworked, stressed, little contact with other people, lack of sexual fulfillment, etc.). The condition is simply described as "the flab caused by overeating because of emotional problems." A large number of these people, especially women, grow fat because they try to solve their psychological conflicts by eating, drinking or nibbling sweets. The excessive intake of food and drink represents a kind of substitute. Housewives who do not want to waste anything often eat the leftovers. There is also the "nightcap" and eating any leftovers.

Symptoms: At first you may not notice anything, then suddenly your clothes are too tight, a reminder that you have put on weight. This is followed by becoming short of breath and intense sweating when climbing stairs, which requires a greater effort. Standing for any length of time becomes unpleasant and results in flat and aching feet. Even walking on the level, the overweight person can no longer move swiftly and tires quickly. The need for sleep thus increases and the metabolism is slowed down even further. The carbohydrates which are not used up are stored in the body as fatty deposits. In the end a vicious circle develops which can only be broken with great difficulty.

Therapy: With the help of healing magnetic treatment the vegetative nervous system must first be stabilized. In addition to this, the burning off of fat should be stimulated to a greater extent.

General treatment: Negative.

Special treatment: Local, positive part strokes clockwise over the upper and lower part of the stomach region.

Supplementary measures: It makes sense to reduce the excessive consumption of high calorie food for the duration of the cure (fatty, meat, sweets, beans, etc.), as well as alcoholic drinks, and to become more calorie conscious. The loss of weight should be slow and gradual. A rapid loss of weight has a detrimental effect upon the metabolism and general well-being, and often does more harm than good. During the day drink positively magnetized water. Before going to bed take a negatively activated bath.

PAIN IN THE SHOULDER

These pains refer to a variety of complaints which manifest themselves in the shoulder area, the shoulder joint and the upper arm.

Causes: In addition to rheumatic complaints, illnesses of the organs in the chest and the abdomen (e.g., the lungs, heart, pleura, gallbladder) may cause an irritating condition which manifests itself in nervous pains in the areas of the shoulder, arm and neck. If the condition remains untreated, these pains can be accompanied by the hardening or atrophy of the muscles, and in severe cases, even by changes in the bones. That is why a diagnosis is absolutely essential.

Symptoms: The pain radiates from the shoulder, the neck and the inside of the upper arm, over the elbow to the hand. Usually the left side is affected, though in some cases the right side can be affected too.

General treatment: Positive.

Special treatment: Positive, localized, partial strokes over the painful side, starting off in the region of the neck. Then slowly stroke out over the upper and lower arm. Bring the hands back in a curve; repeat the manipulation several times.

Supplementary measures: Place hot compresses with positively activated water on the shoulder and the upper arm.

PANCREAS

The pancreas is a very important organ which has a double function. First it produces important digestive juices which are excreted into the duodenum and play a major role in breaking the food into its basic components: protein, fats and carbohydrates. Secondly, it produces important hormones: these are transmitted to the blood, above all, the vital insulin which is responsible for the sugar level in the blood. Any disease of this organ can be fatal.

Cause: The excretion of the digestive juices is controlled by the vegetative nervous system, i.e., we cannot exert any influence over it either consciously or unconsciously. Malfunctions may be caused by incorrect nervous functioning, as well as by disorders in the small intestine. We are not going to dwell here on the acute inflammation of the pancreas (pancreatitis), since this is a serious illness and must without fail be treated clinically, and thus requires admittance to hospital.

Symptoms: Disturbances in the functioning of the pancreas are usually first noticed by a difficulty in digesting certain foods, and in the excreted feces (oily, with undigested muscle fibers and an unpleasant smell). Excessive flatulence may also point to a functional disorder of the pancreas. The symptoms of acute pancreatitis include intense stomach pains, nausea, vomiting and poor circulation.

General treatment: Positive.

Special treatment: Stomach hold.

Supplementary measures: Food should always be well chewed and masticated. Food that is difficult to digest and that causes flatulence should be avoided. It is also advisable not to consume alcohol. Drink positively magnetized water.

POOR CIRCULATION IN THE BRAIN

This is usually a symptom of old age. Our life expectancy is constantly rising, and thus the calcification of the arteries of the brain (cerebral sclerosis) also increase as an independent symptom.

Causes: Two main factors play a part in this condition: the reduced performance of the heart due to age and the calcification of the arteries. Because of deposits on the walls of the arteries, the un-impeded flow of blood is no longer guaranteed. In addition, the supplying arteries may become narrower as a consequence of the over-stimulation of the sympathetic nervous system.

Symptoms: The illness usually starts with forgetfulness and a lack of concentration. Other symptoms include dizziness, shaking, clumsi-ness, confusion and senseless activities. In addition, changes in personality are not uncommon: otherwise quiet people become aggressive and lacking in self-control.

General treatment: Positive.

Special treatment: Radiation of the forehead, followed by the laying on of the hands on the head for about one minute.

Supplementary measures: Medical treatment should not be stopped.

PREGNANCY COMPLAINTS

During pregnancy, which normally lasts approximately 263-270 days, many women suffer from a variety of complaints which may be very unpleasant.

Causes: Physical and psychological problems may arise because of the change in the organism to increase its performance, and because the womb increases in size and exerts pressure on the adjoining organs (stomach, bladder, intestines). Thus there may be malfunc-tions of the internal secretory glands, impaired circulation of the blood and an increased strain on the heart because of the larger volume of blood required. In addition, the veins may become weaker, and possibly result in hemorrhoids or varicose veins.

Symptoms: During the first three months of pregnancy women often suffer from nausea, loss of appetite, dizziness, voracious hunger, or a desire for extremely unusual foods, whereas they may suddenly develop a strong aversion to foods which were favorites before pregnancy. Changes in the skin are also possible. During the last three months of the pregnancy there are frequent stomach aches, troubles with the bowels and a constant need to pass water.

Therapy: As it is assumed that all pregnant women are under medical supervision nowadays, and are well cared for in pre-natal clinics, healing magnetism merely serves to soothe the troubles which accompany pregnancy.

General treatment: Positive. If necessary, it is sufficient to carry out one magnetic session of about ten minutes per week.

RHEUMATIC COMPLAINTS

The word "rheumatism" is derived from the Greek word meaning "to flow," because the illness usually attacks several places in turn, i.e., it flows through the body. Since there are a large number of symptoms all classified under the term "rheuma," in modern medicine they are all referred to as rheumatic complaints. Over the years the illness has become widespread and gigantic sums of money are spent to cure the problem.

Cause: There is still no consensus of opinion regarding the causes of the disease. However, it is certain that acute rheumatism, or rheumatic fever, is closely linked to the infection caused by bacteria (streptococcus). In addition, the patient's condition and predisposition towards illness also play a part. Another form of illness arises from degenerative changes of the joints or the vertebral column. In the case of acute inflammation of the joints, the condition is called arthritis. Muscles too may be attacked by rheumatism. In this case inflamed nerves or nerve pathways are responsible. Disturbance in the hormonal balance (colds or allergies) may also be responsible.

Symptoms: The symptoms of rheumatic fever include pain, swelling and redness of the medium and larger joints (knee, shoulder, elbow, wrist), accompanied by a fever. It is characteristic that at first only one joint is affected for a short time. The illness then passes to another joint. In addition, loss of appetite, shivering and sweating can occur. Another danger is that the heart may become damaged. When the complaint becomes chronic, the rheuma nodules, the thickening of the joints of the fingers and hands, become clearly visible.

In other forms of rheumatism there are long lasting and increasing pains in the various joints which impede the patient's mobility. In the case of fibrositis, these pains mainly affect the muscles in the upper and lower arm around the shoulders, the small of the back and the thighs. The symptoms of rheumatic complaints are so varied that it is impossible to give a description of them all. A doctor must be consulted.

Therapy: Healing magnetic treatment can above all be used for soothing the pain. The affected parts of the body are treated several times a day with localized partial strokes for about three to five minutes. There should be a break of about two hours between each session.

General treatment: Positive.

Supplementary measures: Place hot compresses with positively magnetized water on the parts of the body affected. Change the poultices frequently.

SCIATICA

The nerve of the hip (nervus ischiadicus) runs through the buttocks, along the backside of the thigh, through the kneecaps and calves, down to the lateral regions of the feet. In these regions the main strand has numerous ramifications which are only absent from the front and the inside of the thigh and the inside edge of the foot. The region to which the pain may spread is correspondingly large. Sciatica is therefore very common.

Cause: Since the nerve and its branches run fairly close to the surface, it is particularly susceptible to colds and injuries. Moreover, damage to the interarticular discs may, if it arises in the region of the roots of the nerves, provoke sciatic pains. Excessive consumption of nicotine and alcohol can lead to attacks of sciatica. The same applies to various poisons (lead, mercury), metabolic diseases and infections.

Symptoms: The pain usually starts slowly and only in certain parts of the path of the nerve, mostly on the back of the thigh where the nerve leaves the pelvis. Then it increases in intensity, and finally it seizes the entire region of the path of the nerve. During the night the pain is felt more intensely; in addition, prolonged standing or exercise increase the pain. The patient finds it difficult to walk and he prefers to remain in a certain resting position. Usually the sciatica appears on one side, rarely on both sides.

General treatment: Negative.

Special treatment: The patient lies on his stomach. With the cross grip, slow negative strokes are applied with the hands crossed over following the course of the sciatic nerve: from the small of the back, over the buttocks to the kneecaps, and from there further down to the heels.

Supplementary measures: Good results are achieved with neural and segmental therapy, as well as intramuscular injections of vitamin B complex. The use of these remedies may only be prescribed and carried out by authorized practitioners. Bathing in positively magnetized water has a supportive effect.

SENSITIVITY TO WEATHER CHANGES

In recent years, meteoropathology, the science of the influence of the weather upon people, has received an increasing amount of attention. It is nowadays well-known that the weather may appreciably impair our general well-being, mood, behavior to the world about us, reactions and adaptability to unforeseen situations.

Causes: Changes in temperature, atmospheric humidity and pressure, climate, sudden changes from cold to warm and vice-versa (warm and cold fronts), extremely windy weather, etc., affect the nervous system. In some cases this may result in a slackening or tensing up of the vascular nerves which can, in turn, cause changes in the circulation. Sensitive people may find that certain nerves or nerve fibers may also react directly, and this manifests itself in painful symptoms.

Symptoms: "The weather's changing." Many people suffering from rheumatism, amputated limbs, large scars or bone fractures feel when the weather is going to change. Their prediction is usually reliable, for these people suffer from the pains concerned, even before the weather changes.

Generally healthy people with a rather delicate constitution may be susceptible to the weather in the form of feeling unwell, irritability, lack of concentration, decline in performance, constant yawning, delayed reactions, reluctance to work, headaches, vertigo, tiredness or similar symptoms with no recognizable organic cause. Sensitivity to changes in the weather is not related to either sex.

According to the most recent findings, electric fields preceding the change of climate by some hundreds of miles are responsible for these symptoms. That is why sensitive people feel the oncoming change in the weather in advance, even if a change does not seem likely.

General treatment: Negative.

Special treatment: Depending on the individual complaint, apply the corresponding strokes; for example, in the case of headaches, nervousness, etc., use the forehead stroke. In the case of problems with circulation, treat for the heart; with dizziness treat for the ear, etc.

SLIPPED DISC

The "slipped disc" has become a common expression. The disc itself is a cartilaginous link between two vertebrae of the spinal column. These fibrous cartilaginous rings between the vertebrae fulfill an important function. Without them the elasticity of the spinal column would be considerably reduced in its important function of supporting and movement—each step or movement we made would be unpleasant and painful for us.

Cause: Through the continuous overstraining of the vertebral column, the discs are exposed to pressure and are therefore subjected to premature wear and tear. This frequently causes a slipped disc. Depending on the size of the dislocated tissue, pressure on the spinal column or on the dislocated nerve ends results in severe pain which naturally is followed by immobility, and frequently also limping or other pathological deficiencies. Only a specialist can establish where and in which part of the vertebral column the problem is situated. Don't try to alter the condition with magnetic therapy—the patient should see a specialist for this.

Symptoms: Pains in the area of the vertebral column, in the arms and legs, around the shoulders, in the neck and the head, and tiredness which is felt in the small of the back, may result from an injury to a disc, as well as pains in the chest and in the heart region. (Pains in the heart do not always necessarily mean that there is a heart condition.) That is why it is impossible to diagnose the condition oneself, and no attempt should be made to do so.

Therapy: healing magnetism has a supportive role.

General treatment: Positive.

Special treatment: The patient lies on his stomach. With the cross grip, the practitioner carries out slow positive strokes on both sides of the vertebral column from the region of the coccyx to the area of the neck.

Supplementary measures: Chiropractic, neural therapy, and injections of symphytum preparations, administered by trained doctors or healing practitioners, usually provide great relief. Baths with positively magnetized water have a soothing effect.

STOMACH PAINS/ULCERS, GASTRITIS

Many people suffer from stomach complaints. With healthy people, pressure on the stomach that results from overeating passes after a short time. However, frequently there are also stomach pains with an empty stomach, and these can be particularly severe. The stomach fulfills the important function of a collective tank into which the food passes from the mouth, through the gullet, and where it is first broken up by the gastric acids and other digestive juices.

Causes: Frequently the natural function of the stomach is unable to cope with the excessive quantities of food entering it. With increasing age a weakness of the enzyme production may also be responsible. One of the most common reasons has a psychological origin; others can be traced to the consumption of too many or too strong substances, e.g., alcohol or nicotine. It is commonly believed that anger goes straight to the stomach. This is undoubtedly correct, since this "gut feeling" does not always need to manifest itself as nausea or loss of appetite, but may also cause inflammations of the mucous membrane of the stomach, or even ulcers of the stomach and the duodenum (ulcus duodenalis).

Symptoms: The pains occur mainly between the navel and the sternum, especially in the pit of the stomach. If there is an inflammation of the mucous membrane, or if the duodenum is inflamed as well, the pain subsides after eating, and recurs only two or three hours later. In the case of a nervous stomach or psychological strain, the stomach pain is independent of the intake of food and often occurs spontaneously with a sharp, piercing sensation, sometimes in the form of colic. It is up to the doctor to establish the precise cause (X-rays, gastroscopy, examination of the acids, etc.).

General therapy: Negative.

Special treatment: Stomach stroke.

Supplementary measures: Drink negatively magnetized water. Twice a week, before going to bed, have a negatively radiated bath.

VARICOSE VEINS

Women are most affected by varicose veins, which often appear after a pregnancy. Nevertheless, there are also men who suffer from them, especially if they have to stand a lot in their work, e.g., people in retail sales. Varicose veins cannot always be seen, though the veins on the calves or the thighs near the surface push outwards and thus become visible. There are also deeper veins which are not visible externally when they are cramped up, but which can still cause the same suffering.

Cause: In most cases it is an inherent weakness of the connective tissues. Thus there is an inherited predisposition to the condition. It may also be caused by the inefficient functioning of the valves of the veins. The suffering is caused or exacerbated by constant activity, pregnancy, overweight and lack of exercise.

Symptoms: Externally visible varicose veins are a very familiar condition; tortuous, protruding, bluish veins on the calves, sometimes as thick as a finger, and occasionally also found on the backs of the feet or the thigh.

At first, varicose veins are only reported as a blemish, and they cause hardly any trouble. With increasing weakness of the veins, there is a feeling of heaviness in the legs, frequently accompanied by dragging, convulsive pains; at a more advanced stage there is swelling on the backs of the feet and the ankles. In particularly severe cases, the veins break open and turn into wounds which do not heal easily (ulcus cruris).

Therapy: Healing magnetic treatment can only have a supportive function here.

General treatment: Positive.

Special treatment: The patient lies down, and localized, partial strokes are administered with the hands crossed over, from the heels, over the back of the knee to the buttocks. In addition, it is extremely important to exercise the connective tissues.

Supplementary measures: It is important to wear support stockings or pressure bandages, wrapping the limb concerned with elastic bandages. In particularly severe cases, the surgical removal of the varicose veins by a specialist doctor should be considered.

VERTIGO

Vertigo is a common and unpleasant side effect of many illnesses. Therefore vertigo should always be examined medically. Nearly everybody has at some point, for some reason, experienced a feeling of sudden dizziness.

Causes: The causes of vertigo include extremely vigorous turning and falling movements, as well as unusual changes of balance (e.g., in a boat, fairground, etc.) and sudden variations of the accustomed atmospheric pressure (mountain climbing, trips in aircraft). In addition, poor circulation to the brain (high or low blood pressure) can also be responsible for vertigo in some people. Illnesses of the inner ear (labyrinth) frequently cause vertigo. Head injuries, alcohol and nicotine abuse, vegetative disorders, food poisoning and some infectious diseases can also trigger off attacks of dizziness. We do not have the space to cover all the possible causes here.

Symptoms: The patient feels as if the ground were rocking. The sense of balance is disturbed (rocking vertigo). Another form is turning vertigo. In this case one feels that the ground is moving. Usually conditions of dizziness are accompanied by discomfort, sickness, outbreaks of sweating or vomiting.

Therapy: Depending on the cause established by a medical examination, the fundamental problem should always be treated. For temporary relief, a negative general treatment may be carried out until the factors responsible for the vertigo have been determined.

WEIGHTLOSS

The body weight depends on age, height, combinations of foods and glandular activity. As a norm for a man, if someone is 5 feet 5 inches tall, his normal weight might be 150 pounds. Women who have a lighter bone structure would weigh correspondingly less.

However, this yardstick can only be used with some reservations since, depending on predisposition and heredity, there are athletic women and slender men. According to Kretschmer, the three most characteristic types of body are the leptosome type, the pycnic and the athletic type. In addition, there are many people who do not belong to a particular category, but are to some extent a mixture of the three types.

The body weight of the healthy person is always subject to small variations, which are completely normal, and depend on food intake and physical activity. If someone loses weight and also feels weak and sick, this usually means that something is wrong. A thorough examination is urgently needed.

Cause: First of all, the cause of a loss in weight should always be examined medically because serious illness, often with life endangering consequences, can be concealed by a progressive loss of weight.

Many people are unable to eat sufficiently, or do not eat adequately for psychological reasons (they have no appetite), and they lose weight as a result. Worries of a personal or business nature which burden you, in the long run spoil your appetite. The best known form of this symptom is lovesickness, to which not only younger people, but also the old succumb. ("There's no fool like an old fool.")

Symptoms: The loss of weight due to psychological reasons should nearly always be considered in the context of the problems causing it. If the general emotional condition improves, the appetite will usually improve, too, and the patient will gain weight as long as the organs and the glands are functioning normally. Apart from stimulating the appetite, the vegetative nervous system must also be stabilized.

General treatment: Positive for loss of weight as a result of illness or for organic reasons.

Special treatment: Stomach stroke.

General treatment: Negative for loss of weight for nervous reasons.

Special treatment: Forehead stroke.

Additional measures: For the period of treatment any excitement should be avoided; the patient should not watch exciting films or attend busy functions. Excessive physical strain should be avoided, as well as hurried eating. Regular sleep is also very important. For loss of weight resulting from a psychological condition, drink negatively magnetized water, when there are other reasons, drink positively magnetized water.

BIBLIOGRAPHY

Bittel, Karl. *The Famous Herr Doctor Mesmer from Lake Constance.* Alten: Otto Walter AG, 1957.

Blavatsky, H.P. *Isis Unveiled.* Wheaton, IL: Theosophical Publishing House, 1971.

Blume, Dr. G. "Medicine in Ancient Egypt" in *Cesra-Saule,* Vol. 17 and 23. Baden-Baden, 1982.

Bondegger, Harry W. *Knowledge about Personal Magnetism.* Freiburg: Rudolph'sche Publishers' Bookshop.

Brandler-Bracht. *Textbook on the Development of Occult Forces.* Leipzig: Max Altmann Publishers, 1920.

Braun, Friederich Eduard. *The Healing Power of Vital Magnetism.* Bad Schmiedeberg and Leipzig: F.E. Baumann, 1905.

Brockhaus, F.A. *The New Brockhaus.* Wiesbaden, 1974.

Chertok, Dr. Leon. *Hypnosis.* Ghent: Ramon F. Keller, 1970.

Gleichmann, Dr. Oskar. "The Pulsating Magnetic Field and Its Relevance to the Treatment of Serious Illnesses," in *Weather, Earth, Man,* a periodical of the Research Circle for Geobiology. Eberbach, 1978.

Gratzinger, Dr. Josef. *The Magnetic Healing Procedure: Handbook for Doctors and Laymen.* Vienna and Leipzig, 1900.

Haag, Herbert. *Bible Lexicon.* Zurich-Koln: Benzinger Publishers, 1951.

Jurgens, Heinrich. *How Do I Magnetize?* Freiburg: Hermann Bauer Publishers, 1952.

Keidel, Dr. Wolf. *Concise Textbook of Physiology.* Stuttgart: Georg Thieme Publishers, 1967.

Klein, Adolf and Gerling, Reinhold. *Healing Magnetism.* Oranienburg: Orania Publishers, 1911.

Kramer, Philipp Walburg. *Healing Magnetism: Its Theory and Practices.* Landshut: Krull'sche University Bookshop, 1874.

Lehmann, Alfred. *Superstition and Magic*. Aalen: Scientica Publishers, 1969.

Mellor, Alec. *The Medical Application of Magnetism*. Wiesbaden, 1982.

Miers, Horst E. *Lexicon of Secret Knowledge*. Freiburg: Hermann Bauer KG, 1970.

Pract. *Bible Handbook*. Kath. Stuttgart: Bibel-Werk Publishers, 1941.

Pschyrembel, Willibad. *Clinical Dictionary*. Berlin-New York: De Gruyter Publishers, 1977.

Reichenbach, Dr. Karl Freiherr von. *Odic Magnetic Letters*. Leipzig: Max Altmann Publishers, 1921.

_____. *Odic Occurrences*. Leipzig: Max Altmann Publishers, 1921.

Schiegel, Heinz. *Color Therapy—Healing through the Force of Colors*. Freiburg: Hermann Bauer Publishers, 2nd edition, 1982.

_____. "Sun, Light and Colors: Color Therapy," in *Nature Healing Practice*, Vol. 24. Munich, 1977.

Schroedter, Willy. *Critical Scientific Experiments*. Freiburg: Hermann Bauer Publishers, 1979.

_____. *New Excursion into the Fantastic*. Freiburg: Hermann Bauer Publishers, 1967.

Schuetz-Rothschuh. *Constitution and Physique of the Human Body*. Munich-Berlin-Vienna: Urban & Schwarzenberg, 1971.

Spiesberger, Karl. *The Aura in Man*. Freiburg: Hermann Bauer, 1983.

Tenhaeff, W.H.C. *Extraordinary Healing Forces*. Alten: Otto Walter Publishers AG, 1957.

Thetter, Rudolf. *Magnetism—The Original Healing Remedy*. Leipzig-Maehr.-Ostrau: Julius Kittls Nachfolger, 1937.

Wiedenmann, Johann Baptist. *The Original Healing Science of Magnetism*. Leipzig: Max Spohr Publishers, 1912.

INDEX